D0915666

The Crisis in the German Social-Democracy

by

ROSA LUXEMBURG

NEW YORK

Howard Fertig

1969

First published in English in 1918

HOWARD FERTIG, INC. EDITION 1969

Library of Congress Catalog Card Number: 68-9607

Grateful acknowledgment is hereby made to The Newberry Library for permission to use its copy of *The Crisis in German Social Democracy* in reproducing the present edition of this work.

PRINTED IN THE UNITED STATES OF AMERICA
BY NOBLE OFFSET PRINTERS, INC.

CONTENTS

THE CRISIS IN THE GERMAN SOCIAL-DEMOCRACY

CHAPTER I.

The scene has thoroughly changed. The six weeks' march to Paris has become a world drama. Mass murder has become a monotonous task, and yet the final solution is not one step nearer. Capitalist rule is caught in its own trap, and cannot ban the spirit that it has invoked.

Gone is the first mad delirium. Gone are the patriotic street demonstrations, the chase after suspicious looking automobiles, the false telegrams, the cholera-poisoned wells. Gone the mad stories of Russian students who hurl bombs from every bridge of Berlin, or Frenchmen flying over Nuremberg; gone the excesses of a spy-hunting populace, the singing throngs, the coffee-shops with their patriotic songs; gone the violent mobs, ready to denounce, ready to persecute women, ready to whip themselves into a delirious frenzy over every wild rumor; gone the atmosphere of ritual murder, the Kishineff air that left the policeman at the corner as the only remaining representative of human dignity.

The show is over. The curtain has fallen on trains filled with reservists, as they pull out amid the joyous cries of enthusiastic maidens. We no longer see their laughing faces, smiling cheerily from the train windows upon a war-mad population. Quietly they trot through the streets, with their sacks upon their shoulders. And the public, with a fretful face, goes about its daily task.

Into the disillusioned atmosphere of pale daylight there rings a different chorus; the hoarse croak of the hawks and hyenas of the battlefield. Ten thousand tents, guaranteed according to specifications, 100,000 kilo of bacon, cocoa powder, coffee substitute, cash on immediate delivery. Shrapnell, drills, ammunition bags, marriage bureaus for war widows, leather belts, war orders—only serious propositions considered. And the cannon fodder that was loaded upon the trains in August and September is rotting on the battlefields of Belgium and the Vosges, while profits are springing, like weeds, from the fields of the dead.

Business is flourishing upon the ruins. Cities are turned into shambles, whole countries into deserts, villages into cemeteries, whole nations into beggars, churches into stables; popular rights, treaties, alliances, the holiest words and the highest authorities have been torn into scraps; every sovereign by the grace of God is called a fool, an unfaithful wretch, by his cousin on the other side; every diplomat calls his colleague in the enemy's country a desperate criminal; each government looks upon the other as the evil genius of its people, worthy only of the contempt of the world. Hunger revolts in Venetia, in Lisbon, in Moscow, in Singapore, pestilence in Russia, misery and desperation everywhere.

Shamed, dishonored, wading in blood and dripping with filth, thus capitalist society stands. Not as we usually see it, playing the roles of peace and righteousness, of order, of philosophy, of ethics—as a roaring beast, as an orgy of anarchy, as a pestilential breath, devastating culture and humanity—so it appears in all its hideous nakedness.

And in the midst of this orgy a world tragedy has occurred; the capitulation of the Social-Democracy. To close one's eyes to this fact, to try to hide it, would be the most foolish, the most dangerous thing that the international proletariat could do. "The Democrat (i. e. the revolutionary middle-class)" says Karl Marx, "emerges from the most shameful downfall as spotlessly as he went innocently into it. With the strengthened confidence that he must win, he is more than ever certain that he and his party need no new principles, that events and conditions must finally come to meet them." Gigantic as his problems are his mistakes. No firmly fixed plan, no orthodox ritual that holds good for all times, shows him the path that he must travel. Historical experience is his only teacher, his Via Dolorosa to freedom is covered not only with unspeakable suffering, but with countless mistakes. The goal of his journey, his final liberation, depends entirely upon the proletariat, on whether *it* understands to learn from *its* own mistakes. Selfcriticism, cruel, unsparing criticim that goes to the very root of the evil is life and breath for the proletarian movement. The catastrophe into which the world has thrust the socialist proletariat is an unexampled misfortune for humanity. But Socialism is lost only if the international proletariat is unable to measure the depths of the catastrophe and refuses to understand the lesson that it teaches.

The last forty-five years in the development of the labor movement are at stake. The present situation is a closing of its accounts, a summing up of the items of half a century of work. In the grave of the Paris Commune lies buried the first phase of the European labor movement and the first International. Instead of spontaneous revolution, revolts, and barricades, after each of which the proletariat relapsed once more into its dull passiveness, there came the systematic daily struggle, the utilization of bourgeois parliamentarism, mass organization, the welding of the economic with the political struggle, of socialist ideals with the stubborn defense of most immediate interests. For the first time the cause of the proletariat and its emancipation were led by the guiding star of scientific knowledge. In place of sects and schools, utopian undertakings and experiments in every country, each altogether and absolutely separate from each other, we found a uniform, international, theoretical basis, that united the nations. The theoretical works of Marx gave to the working-class of the whole world a compass by which to fix its tactics from hour to hour, in its journey toward the one unchanging goal.

The bearer, the defender, the protector of this new method was

the German Social-Democracy. The war of 1870 and the downfall of the Paris Commune had shifted the centre of gravity of
the European labor movement to Germany. Just as France was
the classic country of the first phase of the proletarian class-
struggle, as Paris was the torn and bleeding heart of the European
working-class of that time, so the German working-class became
the vanguard of the second phase. By innumerable sacrifices in
the form of agitational work it has built up the strongest, the
model organization of the proletariat, has created the greatest
press, has developed the most effective educational and propaganda methods. It has collected under its banners the most
gigantic labor masses, and has elected the largest representative
groups to its national parliament.

The German Social-Democracy has been generally acknowl-
edged to be the purest incarnation of Marxian Socialism. It has
held and wielded a peculiar prestige as teacher and leader in the
second International. Friedrich Engels wrote in his famous fore-
word to Marx's "Class-Struggle in France": "Whatever may
occur in other countries, the German Social-Democracy occupies
a particular place and, for the present at least, has therefore a
particular duty to perform. The two million voters that it sends
to the ballot boxes, and the young girls and women who stand
behind them as non-voters, are numerically the greatest, the most
compact mass, the most decisive force of the proletarian international army." The German Social-Democracy was, as the "Wiener
Arbeiter-Zeitung" wrote on August 5th, 1914, the jewel of the
organization of the classconscious proletariat. In its footsteps
the French, the Italian and the Belgian Social Democracies, the
labor movements of Holland, Scandinavia, Switzerland and
United States followed more or less eagerly. The Slav nations,
the Russians and the Social-Democrats of the Balkan looked up
to the German movement in boundless, almost unquestioning ad-
miration. In the second International the German Social-Democracy was the determining factor. In every congress, in the

meetings of the International Socialist Bureau, everything waited upon the opinion of the German group.

Particularly in the fight against militarism and war the position taken by the German Social-Democracy has always been decisive. "We Germans cannot accept that," was usually sufficient to determine the orientation of the International. Blindly confident, it submitted to the leadership of the much admired, mighty German Social-Democracy. It was the pride of every Socialist, the horror of the ruling classes of all countires.

And what happened in Germany when the great historical crisis came? The deepest fall, the mightiest cataclysm. Nowhere was the organization of the proletariat made so completely subservient to imperialism. Nowhere was the state of siege so uncomplainingly borne. Nowhere was the press so thoroughly gagged, public opinion so completely choked off; nowhere was the political and industrial class-struggle of the working-class so entirely abandoned as in Germany.

But the German Social-Democracy was not only the strongest body, it was the thinking brain of the International as well. Therefore the process of self-analysis and appraisement must begin in its own movement, with its own case. It is in honor bound to lead the way to the rescue of international Socialism, to proceed with the unsparing criticism of its own shortcomings.

No other party, no other class in capitalist society can dare to expose its own errors, its own weaknesses, before the whole world in the clear mirror of reason, for the mirror would reflect the historical fate that is hidden behind it. The working-class can always look truth in the face even when this means bitterest self-accusation; for its weakness was but an error and the inexorable laws of history give it strength and assure its final victory.

This unsparing self-criticism is not only a fundamental necessity, but the highest duty of the working-class as well. We have on board the highest treasure of humarity, and the proletariat is their ordained protector. While capitalist society, shamed and dishonored, rushes through the bloody orgy to its doom, the international proletariat will gather the golden treasures that were allowed to sink to the bottom in the wild whirlpool of the world-war in the moment of confusion and weakness.

One thing is certain. It is a foolish delusion to believe that we need only live through the war, as a rabbit hides under the bush to await the end of a thunderstorm, to trot merrily off in his old accustomed gait when all is over. The world-war has changed the condition of our struggle, and has changed *us* most of all. Not that the laws of capitalist development or the life and death conflict between capital and labor have been changed or minimized. Even now, in the midst of the war, the masks are falling, and the old well-known faces grinning at us. But evolution has received a mighty forward impetus through the outbreak of the imperialist volcano. The enormity of the tasks that tower before the socialist proletariat in the immediate future make the past struggles of the labor movement seem but a delightful idyll in comparison.

Historically the war is ordained to give to the cause of labor a mighty impetus. Marx, whose prophetic eyes foresaw so many historic events as they lay in the womb of the future, writes, in "The Class-Struggle in France," the following significant passage: "In France the middle class does what should normally be done by the industrial bourgeoisie (i. e. to fight for the democratic republic); but who shall solve the problems of labor? They will not be solved in France. They will be proclaimed in France. They will nowhere be solved within national boundaries. Class war in France will revert into a world war. The solution will begin only when the world war has driven the proletariat into the leadership of that nation which controls the world market, to the leadership of England. The revolution that will here find, not its end, but its organizatory beginning, is no short-lived one. The present generation is like the Jews who were led by

Moses through the wilderness. Not only must it conquer a new world, it must go down to make way for those who will be better able to cope with its problems."

This was written in 1850, at a time when England was the only capitalistically developed nation, when the English proletariat was the best organized and seemed destined through the industrial growth of its nation to take the leadership in the international labor movement. Read Germany instead of England, and the words of Karl Marx become an inspired prohpecy of the present world war. It is ordained to drive the German proletariat "to the leadership of the people, and thus to create the organizatory beginning of the great international conflict between labor and capital for the political supremacy of the world."

Have we ever had a different conception of the role to be played by the working-class in the great world-war? Have we forgotten how we were wont to describe the coming event, only a few short years ago? "Then will come the catastrophe. All Europe will be called to arms, and sixteen to eighteen million men, the flower of the nations, armed with the best instruments of murder will make war upon each other. But I believe that behind this march there looms the final crash. Not we, but they themselves will bring it. They are driving things to the extreme, they are leading us straight into a catastrophe. They will harvest what they have sown. The *Goetterdaemmerung* of the bourgeois world is at hand. Be sure of that. It is coming." Thus spoke Bebel, the speaker of our group in the Reichstag in the Morocco debate.

An official leaflet published by the Party, "Imperialism and Socialism," that was distributed in hundreds of thousands of copies only a few years ago, closes with the words: "Thus the struggle against militarism daily becomes more and more clearly a decisive struggle between capital and labor. War, high prices and capitalism—peace, happiness for all, Socialism! Yours is the choice. History is hastening onward toward a decision. The proletariat must work unceasingly at its world mission, must strengthen the power of its organization and the clearness of its understanding. Then, come what will, whether it will succeed, by its power, in saving humanity from the horrible cruelties of the world-war, or whether capitalism shall sink back into history, as it was born, in blood and violence, the historic moment will find the working-class prepared, and preparedness is everything."

The official handbook for socialist voters, in 1911, the date of the last Reichstag elections, contains, on page 42, the following comments on the expected world-war: "Do our rulers and our ruling classes dare to demand this awful thing of the people? Will not a cry of horror, of fury and of indignation fill the country and lead the people to put an end to this murder? Will they not ask: 'For whom and for what? Are we insane that we should be treated thus or should tolerate such treatment?' He who dispassionately considers the possibility of a great European world-war can come to no other conclusion."

"The next European war will be a game of va-banque, whose equal the world has never seen before. It will be, in all probability, the last war."

With such words the Reichstag representatives won their 110 seats in the Reichstag.

When in the summer of 1911 the "Panther" made its spring to Agadir, and the noisy clamor of German imperialists brought Europe to the precipice of war, an international meeting in London, on the 4th of August, adopted the following resolution:

"The German, Spanish, English, Dutch and French delegates of labor organizations hereby declare their readiness to oppose every declaration of war with every means in their power. Every nationality here represented pledges itself, in accordance with the decisions of its national and international congresses to oppose all criminal machinations on the part of the ruling classes."

But when in November, 1912, the International Peace Congress met at Basel, when the long train of labor representatives entered the Minster, a presentiment of the coming hour of fate made them shudder and the heroic resolve took shape in every breast.

The cool, sceptical Victor Adler cried out: "Comrades, it is most important that we here, at the common source of our strength, that we, each and every one of us take from hence the strength to do in his country what he can, through the forms and means that are at his disposal, to oppose this crime of war. And if it should be accomplished, if we should really be able to prevent war, let this be the cornerstone of our coming victory. That is the spirit that animates the whole International.

"And when murder and arson and pestilence sweep over civilized Europe—we can think of it only with horror and indignation, and protests ring from our hearts. And we ask, are the proletarians of today really nothing but sheep to be led mutely to the slaughter?"

Troelstra spoke in the name of the small nations, in the name of the Belgians as well:

"With their blood and with all that they possess the proletariat of the small nations swear their allegiance to the International in everything that it may decide to prevent war. Again we repeat that we expect, when the ruling classes of the large nations call the sons of the proletariat to arms to satiate the lust for power and the greed of their rulers, in the blood and on the lands of the small peoples, we expect that then the sons of the proletariat, under the powerful influence of their proletarian parents and of the proletarian press, will think thrice before they harm us, their friends, in the service of the enemies of culture."

And Jaurès closed his speech, after the anti-war manifesto of the International Bureau had been read:

"The International represents the moral forces of the world! And when the tragic hour strikes, when we must sacrifice ourselves, this knowledge will support and strengthen us. Not lightly, but from the bottom of our hearts we declare that we are ready for all sacrifices!"

It was like a Ruetli pledge. The whole world looked toward the Minster of Basel, where the bells, slowly and solemnly, rang to the approaching great fight between the armies of labor and capital.

On the third of September, 1912, the social-democratic deputy, David, spoke in the German Reichstag:

"That was the most beautiful hour of my life. That I here avow. When the chimes of the Minster rang in the long train of international Social-Democrats, when the red flags were planted in the nave of the church about the altar, when the emissaries of the people were greeted by the peels of the organ that resounded the message of peace, that was an impression that I can never forget . . . .

"You must realize what it was that happened here. The masses have ceased to be willess, thoughtless herds. That is new in the history of the world. Hitherto the masses have always blindly followed the lead of those who were interested in war, who drove the peoples at each others' throats to mass murder. That will stop. The masses have ceased to be the instruments, the yeomen of war profiteers."

A week before the war broke out, on the 26th of July, 1914, the German party papers wrote:

"We are no marionettes; we are fighting with all our might, against a system that makes men the powerless tools of blind circumstances, against this capitalism that is preparing to change Europe, thirsty for peace, into a smoking battlefield. If destruction takes its course, if the determined will for peace of the German, of the international proletariat, that will find expression in the next few days in mighty demonstrations, should not be able to prevent the world-war, then it must be at least, the last war, it must be the *Goetterdaemmerung* of capitalism."

On the 30th of July, 1914, the central organ of the German Social-Democracy cried out:

"The socialist proletariat rejects all responsibility for the events that are being precipitated by a ruling class that is blinded, and on the verge of madness. We know that for us new life will spring from the ruins. But the responsibility falls upon the rulers of today.

"For them it is a question of existence!

"Die Weltgeschichte ist das Weltgericht!"

And then came the awful, the incredible 4th of August, 1914.

Did it *have* to come? An event of such importance cannot be a mere accident. It must have its deep, significant, objective causes. But perhaps these causes may be found in the errors of the leader of the proletariat, the Social-Democracy itself, in the fact that our readiness to fight has flagged, that our courage and our convictions have forsaken us. Scientific Socialism has taught us to recognize the objective laws of historical development. Man does not make history of his own volition, but he makes history nevertheless. The proletariat is dependent in its actions upon the degree of righteousness to which social evolution has advanced. But again, social evolution is not a thing apart from the proletariat; it is in the same measure its driving force and its cause as well as its product and its effect. And though we can no more skip a period in our historical development than a man can jump over his shadow, it lies within our power to accelerate or to retard it.

Socialism is the first popular movement in the world that has set itself a goal and has established in the social life of man a conscious thought, a definite plan, the free will of mankind. For this reason Friedrich Engels calls the final victory of the socialist proletariat a stride by human kind from the animal kingdom into the kingdom of liberty. This step, too, is bound by unalterable historical laws to the thousands of rungs of the ladder of the past with its tortuous, sluggish growth. But it will never be accomplished, if the burning spark of the conscious will of the masses does not spring from the material conditions that have been built up by past development. Socialism will not fall as manna from heaven. It can only be won by a long chain of powerful struggles, in which the proletariat, under the leadership of the Social-Democracy, will learn to take hold of the rudder of society to become, instead of the powerless victim of history, its conscious guide.

Friedrich Engels once said:

"Capitalist society faces a dilemma, either an advance to Socialism or a reversion to barbarism." What does a "reversion to barbarism" mean at the present stage of European civilization? We have read and repeated these words thoughtlessly, without a conception of their terrible import. At this moment one glance about us will show us what a reversion to barbarism in capitalist society means. *This world-war* means a reversion to barbarism. The triumph of imperialism leads to the destruction of culture, sporadically during a modern war, and forever, if the period of world-wars that has just begun is allowed to take its damnable course to the last ultimate consequence. Thus we stand today, as Friedrich Engels prophesied more than a generation ago, before the awful proposition: Either the triumph of imperialism and the destruction of all culture, and, as in ancient Rome, depopulation, desolation, degeneration, a vast cemetery; or, the victory of Socialism, that is, the conscious struggle of the international proletariat against imperialism, against its methods, against war. This is the dilemma of world history, its inevitable choice, whose scales are trembling in the balance, awaiting the decision of the proletariat. Upon it depends the future of culture and humanity. In this war imperialism has been victorious. Its brutal sword of murder has dashed the scales, with overbearing brutality, down into the abyss of shame and misery. If the proletariat learns *from* this war and *in* this war to exert itself, to cast off its serfdom to the ruling classes, to become the lord of its own destiny, the shame and misery will not have been in vain.

The modern working-class must pay dearly for each realization of its historic mission. The road to the Golgotha of its class liberation is strewn with awful sacrifices. The June-combatants, the victims of the Commune, the martyrs of the Russian Revolution—an endless line of bloody shadows. They have fallen on the field of honor, as Marx wrote of the heroes of the Commune, to be enshrined forever in the great heart of the working-class. Now millions of proletarians are falling on the field of dishonor, of fratricide, of self-destruction, the slave-song on their lips. And that, too, has not been spared us. We are like the Jews whom Moses led through the desert. But we are not lost, and we will be victorious if we have not forgotten how to learn. And if the modern leaders of the proletariat do not know how to learn, they will go down "to make room for those who will be more able to cope with the problems of a new world."

CHAPTER II.

"We are now facing the irrevocable fact of war. We are threatened by the horrors of invasion. The decision, today, is not for or against war; for us there can be but one question: By what means is this war to be conducted? Much, aye everything, is at stake for our people and its future, if Russian despotism, stained with the blood of its own people, should be the victor. This danger must be averted, the civilization and the independence of our people must be safeguarded. Therefore we will carry out what we have always promised: In the hour of danger we will not desert our fatherland. In this we feel that we stand in harmony with the International, which has always recognized the right of every people to its national independence, as we stand in agreement with the International in emphatically denouncing every war of conquest. Actuated by these motives, we vote in favor of the war credits demanded by the Government."

With these words the Reichstag group issued the countersign that determined and controlled the position of the German working-class during the war. Fatherland in danger, national defense, people's war for existence, Kultur, liberty—these were the slogans proclaimed by the parliamentary representatives of the Social-Democracy. What followed was but the logical sequence. The position of the Party and the labor union press, the patriotic frenzy of the masses, the civil peace, the disintegration of the International, all these things were the inevitable consequence of that momentous orientation in the Reichstag.

If it is true that this war is really a fight for national existence, for freedom, if it is true that these priceless possessions can be defended only by the iron tools of murder, if this war is the holy cause of the people, then everything else follows as a matter of course, we must take everything that the war may bring as a part of the bargain. He who desires the purpose must be satisfied with the means. War is methodical, organized, gigantic murder. But in normal human beings this systematic murder is possible only when a state of intoxication has been previously created. This has always been the tried and proven method of those who make war. Bestiality of action must find a commensurate bestiality of thought and senses; the latter must prepare and accompany the former. Thus the "Wahre Jacob" of August 28th, 1914, with its brutal picture of the German thresher, the Party papers of Chemnitz, Hamburg, Kiel, Frankfurt a. M., Koburg and others, with their patriotic drive in poetry and prose, were the necessary narcotic for a proletariat that could rescue its existence and its liberty only by plunging the deadly steel into its French and English brothers. These chauvinistic papers are after all a great deal more logical and consistent than those others who attempted to unite hill and valley, war with humanity, murder with brotherly love, the voting for war credits with socialist internationalism.

If the stand taken by the German Reichstag group on the fourth of August was correct, then the death sentence of the proletarian International has been spoken, not only for this war, but for ever. For the first time since the modern labor movement exists there yawns an abyss between the commandments of international solidarity of the proletariat of the world and the interests of freedom and nationalist existence of the people; for the first time we discover that the independence and liberty of the nations command that workingmen kill and destroy each other. Up to this time we have cherished the belief that the interests of the peoples of all nations, that the class interests of the proletariat are a harmonious unit, that they are identical, that they cannot possibly come into conflict with one another. That was the basis of our theory and practice, the soul of our agitation. Were we mistaken in the cardinal point of our whole world philosophy? We are holding an inquest over international Socialism.

This world war is not the first crisis through which our international principles have passed. Our Party was first tried forty-five years ago. At that time, on the 21st of July, 1870, Wilhelm Liebknecht and August Bebel made the following historical declaration before the Reichstag:

"The present war is a dynastic war in the interest of the Bonaparte dynasty, as the war of 1866 was conducted in the interest of the Hohenzollern dynasty.

"We cannot vote for the funds which are demanded from the Reichstag to conduct this war because this would be, in effect, a vote of confidence in the Prussian government. And we know that the Prussian government, by its action in 1866, prepared this war. At the same time we cannot vote against the budget, lest this be construed to mean that we support the conscienceless and criminal policies of Bonaparte.

"As opponents, on principle, of every dynastic war, as Socialist-Republicans and members of the 'International Workingmen's Association' which, without regard to nationality, has fought all oppressors, has tried to unite all the oppressed into a great band of brothers, we cannot directly or indirectly lend support to the present war. We therefore refuse to vote, while expressing the earnest hope that the peoples of Europe, taught by the present unholy events, will strive to win the right to control their own destinies, to do away with the present rule of might and class as the cause of all social and national evil."

With this declaration the representatives of the German proletariat put their cause clearly and unreservedly under the banner of the International and definitely repudiated the war against France as a national war of independence. It is well known that Bebel many years later, in his memoirs, stated that he would have voted against the war loan had he known, when the vote was taken, the things that were revealed in the years that followed.

Thus, in a war that was considered by the whole bourgeois

public, and by a powerful majority of the people under the influence of Bismarckian strategy, as a war in the national life interest of Germany, the leaders of the German Social-Democracy held firmly to the conviction that the life interest of a nation and the class interest of the proletariat are one, that both are opposed to war. It was left to the present world war and to the Social-Democratic Reichstag group to uncover, for the first time, the terrible dilemma—either you are for national liberty—or for international Socialism.

Now the fundamental fact in the declaration of our Reichstag group was, in all probability, a sudden inspiration. It was simply an echo of the crown speech and of the Chancellor's speech of August fourth. "We are not driven by the desire for conquest," we hear in the crown speech, "we are inspired by the unalterable determination to preserve the land upon which God has placed us for ourselves, and for all coming generations. From the documents that have been presented to you, you will have seen how My Government, and above all My Chancellor strove, to the last, to avert the utmost. We grasp the sword in self-defense, with a clear conscience and a clean hand." And Bethmann-Hollweg declared: "Gentlemen, we are acting in self-defense, and necessity knows no law. He who is threatened as we are threatened, he who is fighting for the highest aims can be guided by but one consideration, how best to beat his way out of the struggle. We are fighting for the fruits of our peaceful labor, for the heritage of our great past, for the future of our nation." Wherein does this differ from the social-democratic declaration? 1. We have done everything to preserve peace, the war was forced upon us by others. 2. Now that the war is here we must act in self-defense. 3. In this war the German people is in danger of losing everything. This declaration of our Reichstag group is an obvious rehashing of the government declaration. As the latter based their claims upon diplomatic negotiations and imperial telegrams, so the socialist group points to peace demonstrations of the Social-Democracy before the war. Where the crown speech denies all aims of conquest, the Reichstag group repudiates a war of conquest by standing upon its Socialism. And when the Emperor and the Chancellor cry out, "We are fighting for the highest principles. We know no parties, we know only Germans," the social-democratic declaration echoes: "Our people risks everything. In this hour of danger we will not desert our Fatherland." Only in one point does the social-democratic declaration differ from its government model, it placed the danger of Russian despotism in the foreground of its orientation, as a danger to German freedom. The crown speech says, regarding Russia: "With a heavy heart I have been forced to mobilize against a neighbor with whom I have fought upon so many battle fields. With honest sorrow I have seen a friendship faithfully kept by Germany, fall to pieces." The social-democratic group changed this sorrowful rupture of a true friendship with the Russian Tsar into a fanfare for liberty against despotism, used the revolutionary heritage of Socialism to give to the war a democratic mantle, a popular halo. Here alone the social-democratic declaration gives evidence of independent thought on the part of our Social-Democrats.

As we have said, all these things came to the Social Democracy as a sudden inspiration on the fourth of August. All that they had said up to this day, every declaration that they had made, down to the very eve of the war, was in diametrical opposition to the declaration of the Reichstag group. The "Vorwaerts" wrote on July 25th, when the Austrian ultimatum to Servia was published:

"They want the war, the unscrupulous elements that influence and determine the Wiener Hofburg. They want the war—it has been ringing out of the wild cries of the black-yellow press for weeks. They want the war—the Austrian ultimatum to Servia makes it plain and clear to the world.

"Because the blood of Franz Ferdinand and his wife flowed under the shots of an insane fanatic, shall the blood of thousands of workers and farmers be shed? Shall one insane crime be purged by another even more insane? . . . The Austrian ultimatum may be the torch that will set Europe in flames at all four corners.

"For this ultimatum, in its form and in its demands, is so shameless, that a Servian Government that should humbly retreat before this note, would have to reckon with the possibility of being driven out by the masses of the people between dinner and dessert. . . .

"It was a crime of the chauvinistic press of Germany to egg on our dear Ally to the utmost in its desire for war. And beyond a doubt, Herr von Bethmann-Hollweg promised Herr Berchtold our support. But Berlin is playing a game as dangerous as that being played by Vienna."

The "Leipziger Volkszeitung" wrote on July 24th:

"The Austrian military party has staked everything on one card, for in no country in the world has national and military chauvinism anything to lose. In Austria chauvinistic circles are particularly bankrupt; their nationalistic howls are a frantic attempt to cover up Austria's economic ruin, the robbery and murder of war to fill its coffers . . ."

The "Dresden Volkszeitung" said, on the same day:

"Thus far the war maniacs of the Wiener Ballplatz have failed to furnish proof that would justify Austria in the demands it has made upon Servia. So long as the Austrian Government is not in a position to do this, it places itself, by its provocative and insulting attacks upon Servia, in a false position before all Europe. And even if Servia's guilt was proven, even if the assassination in Serajewo had actually been prepared under the eyes of the Servian Government, the demands made in the note are far in excess of normal bounds. Only the most unscrupulous war lust can explain such demands upon another state. . ."

The "Muenchener Post," on July 25th, wrote:

"This Austrian note is a document unequalled in the history of the last two centuries. Upon the findings of an investigation whose contents have, till now, been kept from the European public, without court proceedings against the murderer of the heir-presumptive and his spouse, it makes demands on Servia, the acceptance of which would mean national suicide to Servia. . ."

The "Schleswig-Holstein Volkszeitung" declared, on the 24th of July:

"Austria is provoking Servia. Austria-Hungary wants war, and is committing a crime that may drown all Europe in blood. . . Austria is playing va banque. It dares a provocation of the Servian state that the latter, if it is not entirely defenseless, will certainly refuse to tolerate. . .

"Every civilized person must protest emphatically against the criminal behavior of the Austrian rulers. It is the duty of the workers above all, and of all other human beings who honor peace and civilization, to try their utmost to prevent the consequences of the bloody insanity that has broken out in Vienna."

The "Magdeburger Volksstimme" of July 25th said:

"Any Servian Government that even pretended to consider these demands seriously would be swept out in the same hour by the Parliament and by the people.

"The action of Austria is the more despicable because Berchtold is standing before the Servian Government and before Europe with empty hands.

"To precipitate a war such as this at the present time, means to invite a world war. To act thus shows a desire to disturb the peace of an entire hemisphere. One cannot thus make moral conquests, or convince non-participants of one's own righteousness. It can be safely assumed that the press of Europe, and with it the European governments, will call the vainglorious and senseless Viennese statesmen energetically and unmistakably to order."

On July 24th the "Frankfurter Volksstimme" wrote:

"Upheld by the agitation of the clerical press, which mourns in Franz Ferdinand its best friend and demands that his death be avenged upon the Servian people, upheld by German war patriots whose language becomes daily more contemptible and more threatening, the Austrian Government has allowed itself to be driven to send an ultimatum to Servia couched in language that, for presumptuousness, leaves little to be desired; containing demands whose fulfillment by the Servian Government is manifestly impossible."

On the same day the "Elberfelder Freie Presse" wrote:

"A telegram of the semi-official Wolf Bureau reports the terms of the demands made on Servia by Austria. From these it may be gathered that the rulers in Vienna are pushing toward war with all their might. For the conditions imposed by the note that was presented in Belgrade last night are nothing short of a protectorate of Austria over Servia. It is eminently necessary that the diplomats of Berlin make the war agitators of Vienna understand that Germany will not move a finger to support such outrageous demands, that a withdrawal of the threats would be advisable."

The "Bergische Arbeiterstimme" of Solingen writes:

"Austria demands a conflict with Servia, and uses the assassination at Serajewo as a pretext for putting Servia morally in the wrong. But the whole matter has been approached too clumsily to influence European public opinion.

"But if the war agitators of the Wiener Ballplatz believe that their allies of the Triple Alliance, Germany and Italy, will come to their assistance in a conflict in which Russia, too, will be involved, they are suffering from a dangerous illusion. Italy would welcome the weakening of Austria-Hungary, its rival on the Adriatic and in the Balkans, and would certainly decline to burn its fingers to help Austria. In Germany, on the other hand, the powers that be—even should they be so foolish as to wish it—would not dare to risk the life of a single soldier to satisfy the criminal lust for power of the Hapsburgers without arousing the fury of the entire people."

Thus the entire working-class press, without exception, judged the war's causes a week before its outbreak. Obviously the question was one of neither the existence nor the freedom of Germany, but a shameful adventure of the Austrian war party; not a question of self-defense, national protection and a holy war forced upon us in the name of freedom, but a bold provocation, an abominable threat against foreign, Servian, independence and liberty.

What was it that happened on August fourth to turn this clearly defined and so unanimously accepted attitude of the Social-Democracy upside down? Only one new factor had appeared—the White Book that was presented to the Reichstag by the German Government on that day. And this contained, on page 4, the following:

"Under these circumstances Austria must say to itself that it is incompatible with the dignity and the safety of the monarchy to remain inactive any longer in face of the occurrences across the border. The Austrian Imperial Government has notified us of this, their attitude, and has begged us to state our views. Out of a full heart we could but assure our Ally of our agreement with this interpretation of conditions and assure him that any action that would seem necessary to put an end to Servian attempts against the existence of the Austrian monarchy would meet with our approval. We fully realized that eventual war measures undertaken by Austria must bring Russia into the situation and that we, in order to carry out our duty as ally, might be driven into war. But we could not, realizing as we did that the most vital interests of Austria-Hungary were threatened, advise our ally to adopt a policy of acquiescence, that could not possibly be brought into accord with its dignity, nor could we refuse to lend our aid in this attitude.

"And we were particularly prevented from taking this stand by the fact that the persistent subversive Serbian agitation seriously jeopardized us. If the Serbians had been permitted, with the aid of Russia and France, to continue to threaten the existence of the neighboring monarchy, there would have ensued a gradual collapse of Austria and a subjection of all the Slavic races under the Russian sceptre, which would have rendered untenable the situation of the Germanic race in Central Europe. A morally weakened Austria, succumbing before the advance of Russian Panslavism, would no longer be an ally on which we could count and depend, as we are obliged to do in view of the increasingly menacing attitude of our neighbors to the East and to the West. We therefore gave Austria a free hand in her proceedings against Serbia. We have had no share in the preparations."

These were the words that lay before the social-democratic Reichstag group on August 4th, the only important and determining phrases in the entire White Book, a concise declaration of the German Government beside which all other yellow, grey, blue, orange books on the diplomatic passages that preceded the war and its most immediate causes become absolutely irrevelant and insignificant. Here the Reichstag group had the key to a correct judgment of the situation in hand. The entire social-democratic press, a week before, had cried out that the Austrian ultimatum was a criminal provocation of the world war and demanded preventative and pacific action on the part of the German Government. The entire socialist press assumed that the Austrian ultimatum had descended upon the German Government like a bolt from the blue as it had upon the German public. But now the White Book declared, briefly and clearly: 1. That the Austrian Government had requested German sanction before taking a final step against Servia. 2. That the German Government clearly understood that the action undertaken by Austria would lead to war with Servia, and ultimately, to European war. 3. That the German Government did not advise Austria to give in, but on the contrary declared that an acquiescent, weakened Austria could not be regarded as a worthy ally of Germany. 4. That the German Government assured Austria, before it advanced against Servia, of its assistance under all circumstances, in case of war, and finally, 5. That the German Government, withal, had not reserved for itself control over the decisive ultimatum from Austria to Servia, upon which the whole world war depended, but had left to Austria "an absolutely free hand."

All of this our Reichstag group learned on August 4th. And still another fact it learned from the Government—that German forces already had invaded Belgium. And from all this the Social-Democratic group concluded that this is a war of defense against foreign invasion, for the existence of the fatherland, for "Kultur," a war for liberty against Russian despotism.

Was the obvious background of the war, and the scenery that so scantily concealed it, was the whole diplomatic performance

that was acted out at the outbreak of the war, with its clamor
about a world of enemies, all threatening the life of Germany,
all moved by the one desire to weaken, to humiliate, to subjugate
the German people and nation—were all these things such a
complete surprise? Did these factors actually call for more
judgment, more critical sagacity than they possessed? Nowhere
was this less true than of our Party. It had already gone through
two great German wars, and in both of them had received memorable lessons.

Even a poorly-informed student of history knows that the war
of 1866 against Austria was systematically prepared by Bismarck
long before it broke out, and that his policies, from the very
beginning, led inevitably to a rupture and to war with Austria.
The Crown Prince himself, the later Emperor Frederick, in his
memoirs under the date of November 14th of that year, speaks
of this purpose of the Chancellor:

"He (Bismarck), when he went into office, was firmly resolved
to bring Prussia to a war with Austria, but was very careful
not to betray this purpose, either at that time or on any other
premature occasion to his Majesty, until the time seemed
favorable."

"Compare with this confession," says Auer in his brochure
'Die Sedanfeier und die Sozialdemokratie,' "the proclamation
that King William sent out 'to my people.' "

"The Fatherland is in danger! Austria and a large part of
Germany have risen in arms against us.

"It is only a few years ago since I, of my own free will, without
thinking of former misunderstandings, held out a fraternal hand
to Austria in order to save a German nation from foreign dom-
ination. But my hopes have been blasted. Austria cannot forget
that its lords once ruled Germany ; it refuses to see in the younger,
more virile Prussia an ally, but persists in regarding it as a dangerous rival. Prussia—so it believes—must be opposed in all its

aims, because whatever favors Prussia harms Austria. The old unholy jealousy has again broken out; Prussia is to be weakened, destroyed, dishonored. All treaties with Prussia are void, German lords are not only called upon, but persuaded, to sever their alliance with Prussia. Wherever we look, in Germany, we are surrounded by enemies whose war cry is—Down with Prussia!"

Praying for the blessings of heaven, King William ordered a general day of prayer and penance for the 18th of July, saying:

"It has not pleased God to crown with success my attempts to preserve the blessings of peace for my people."

Should not the official accompaniment to the outbreak of the war on August 4th have awakened in the minds of our group vivid memories of long remembered words and melodies? Had they completely forgotten their party history?

But not enough! In the year 1870 there came the war with France, and history has united its outbreak with an unforgettable occurrence; the Ems dispatch, a document that has become a classic byword for capitalist-government art in war making, and which marks a memorable episode in our party history. Was it not old Liebknecht, was it not the German Social-Democracy who felt in duty bound, at that time, to disclose these facts and to show to the masses "how wars are made?"

Making war simply and solely for the protection of the Fatherland was, by the way, not Bismarck's invention. He only carried out, with characteristic unscrupulousness, an old, well known and truly international recipe of capitalist statesmanship. When and where has there been a war since so-called public opinion has played a role in governmental calculations, in which each and every belligerent party did not, with a heavy heart, draw the sword from its sheath for the single and sole purpose of defending its Fatherland and its own righteous course from the shameful attacks of the enemy? This legend is as inextricably a part of the game of war as powder and lead. The game is old. Only, that the Social-Democratic Party should play it is new.

CHAPTER III.

Our Party should have been prepared to recognize the real aims of this war, to meet it without surprise, to judge it by its deeper relationship according to their wide political experience. The events and forces that led to August 4th, 1914, were no secrets. The world had been preparing for decades, in broad daylight, in the widest publicity, step by step and hour by hour, for the world war. And if today a number of Socialists threaten with horrible destruction the "secret diplomacy" that has brewed this deviltry behind the scenes, they are ascribing to these poor wretches a magic power that they little deserve, just as the Boto-kude whips his fetish for the outbreak of a storm. The so-called captains of nations are, in this war, as at all times, merely chess-men, moved by all-powerful historic events and forces, on the surface of capitalist society. If ever there were persons capable of understanding these events and occurrences, it was the members of the German Social-Democracy.

Two lines of development in recent history lead straight to the present war. One has its origin in the period when the so-called national states, i. e. the modern states, were first constituted, from the time of the Bismarckian war against France. The war of 1870, which, by the annexation of Alsace-Lorraine, threw the French Republic into the arms of Russia, split Europe into two opposing camps and opened up a period of insane competitive armament, first piled up the fire-brands for the present world conflagration. Bismarck's troops were still stationed in France when Marx wrote to the "Braunschweiger Ausschuss":

"He who is not deafened by the momentary clamor and is not interested in deafening the German people, must see that the war of 1870 carries with it, of necessity, a war between Germany and Russia, just as the war of 1866 bore the war of 1870. I say of necessity, unless the unlikely should happen, unless a revolution breaks out in Russia before that time. If this does not occur, a war between Germany and Russia may even now be regarded as 'un fait accompli.' It depends entirely upon the attitude of the German victor to determine whether this war has been useful or dangerous. If they take Alsace-Lorraine, then France with Russia will arm against Germany. It is superfluous to point out the disastrous consequences."

At that time this prophecy was laughed down. The bonds which united Russia and Prussia seemed so strong that it was considered madness to believe in a union of autocratic Russia with Republican France. Those who supported this conception were laughed at as madmen. And yet everything that Marx has prophesied has happened, to the last letter. "For that is," says Auer in his *Sedanfeier,* "social-democratic politics, seeing things clearly as they are, and differing therein from the day-by-day politics of the others, bowing blindly down before every momentary success."

This must not be misunderstood to mean that the desire for revenge for the robbery accomplished by Bismarck has driven the French into a war with Germany, that the kernel of the present war is to be found in the much discussed "revenge for Alsace-Lorraine." This is the convenient nationalist legend of the German war agitator, who creates fables of a darkly-brooding France that "cannot forget" its defeat, just as the Bismarckian press-savants ranted of the dethroned Princess Austria who could not forget her erstwhile superiority over the charming Cinderella Prussia. As a matter of fact revenge for Alsace-Lorraine has become the theatrical property of a couple of patriotic clowns, the "Lion de Belfort" nothing more than an ancient survival.

The annexation of Alsace-Lorraine long ago ceased to play a role in French politics, being superseded by new, more pressing cares; and neither the government nor any serious party in France thought of a war with Germany because of these territories. If, nevertheless, the Bismarck heritage has become the fire-brand that started this world conflagration, it is rather in the sense of having driven Germany on the one hand, and France, and with it all of Europe, on the other, along the downward path of military competition, of having brought about the Franco-Russian alliance, of having united Austria with Germany as an inevitable consequence. This gave to Russian Czarism a tremendous prestige as a factor in European politics. Germany and France have systematically fawned before Russia for her favor. At that time the links were forged that united Germany with Austria-Hungary, whose strength, as the words quoted from the "White Book" show, lie in their "brotherhood in arms," in the present war.

Thus the war of 1870 brought in its wake the outward political grouping of Europe about the axes of the Franco-German antagonism, and established the rule of militarism in the lives of the European peoples. Historical development has given to this rule and to this grouping an entirely new content. The second line that leads to the present world war, and which again brilliantly justifies Marx's prophecy, has its origin in international occurrences that Marx did not live to see, in the imperialist development of the last 25 years.

The growth of capitalism, spreading out rapidly over a reconstituted Europe after the war period of the 60s and 70s, particularly after the long period of depression that followed the inflation and the panic of the year 1873, reaching an unnatural zenith in the prosperity of the 90s, opened up a new period of storm and danger among the nations of Europe. They were competing in their expansion toward the non-capitalist countries and zones of the world. As early as the 80s a strong tendency toward colonial expansion became apparent. England secured control of Egypt and created for itself, in South Africa, a powerful colonial empire. France took possession of Tunis in North Africa and Tonkin in East Asia; Italy gained a foothold in

Abyssinia; Russia accomplished its conquests in Central Asia and pushed forward into Manchuria; Germany won its first colonies in Africa and in the South Sea, and the United States joined the circle when it procured the Phillipines with "interests" in Eastern Asia. This period of feverish conquests has brought on, beginning with the Chinese-Japanese War in 1895, a practically uninterrupted chain of bloody wars, reaching its height in the great Chinese invasion, and closing with the Russo-Japanese War of 1904.

All these occurrences, coming blow upon blow, created new, extra-European antagonisms on all sides: between Italy and France in Northern Africa, between France and England in Egypt, between England and Russia in Central Asia, between Russia and Japan in Eastern Asia, between Japan and England in China, between the United States and Japan in the Pacific Ocean—a very restless ocean, full of sharp conflicts and temporary alliances, of tension and relaxation, threatening every few years to break out into a war between European powers. It was clear to everybody, therefore, (1) that the secret underhand war of each capitalist nation against every other, on the backs of Asiatic and African peoples must sooner or later lead to a general reckoning, that the wind that was sown in Africa and Asia, would return to Europe as a terrific storm, the more certainly since increased armament of the European States was the constant associate of these Asiatic and African occurrences; (2) that the European world war would have to come to an outbreak as soon as the partial and changing conflicts between the imperialist states found a centralized axis, a conflict of sufficient magnitude to group them, for the time being, into large, opposing factions. This situation was created by the appearance of German imperialism.

In Germany one may study the development of imperialism, crowded as it was into the shortest possible space of time, in concrete form. The unprecedented rapidity of German indus-

trial and commercial development since the foundation of the
Empire, brought out during the 80s two characteristically
peculiar forms of capitalist accumulation; the most pronounced
growth of monopoly in Europe and the best developed and most
concentrated banking system in the whole world. The monopolies have organized the steel and iron industry, i. e., the branch
of capitalist endeavor most interested in government orders, in
militaristic equipment and in imperialistic undertakings (railroad
building, the exploitation of mines, etc.) into the most influential
factor in the nation. The latter has cemented the money interests into a firmly organized whole, with the greatest, most
virile energy, creating a power that autocratically rules the
industry, commerce and credit of the nation, dominant in private
as well as public affairs, boundless in its powers of expansion,
ever hungry for profit and activity, impersonal, and therefore
liberal-minded, reckless and unscrupulous, international by its
very nature, ordained by its capacities to use the world as its
stage.

Germany is under a personal regime, with strong initiative and
spasmodic activity, with the weakest kind of parliamentarism,
incapable of opposition, uniting all capitalist strata in the sharp-
est opposition to the working class. It is obvious that this live,
unhampered imperialism, coming upon the world stage at a time
when the world was practically divided up, with gigantic appetites, soon became an irresponsible factor of general unrest.

This was already foreshadowed by the radical upheaval .that
took place in the military policies of the Empire at the end of
90's. At that time two naval budgets were introduced which
doubled the naval power of Germany and provided for a naval
program covering almost two decades. This meant a sweeping
change in the financial and trade policy of the nation. In the
first place, it involved a striking change in the foreign policy of
the Empire. The policy of Bismarck was founded upon the
principle that the Empire is and must remain a land power, that

the German fleet, at best, is but a very dispensible requisite for coastal defence. Even the secretary of state, Hollmann, declared in March, 1897, in the Budget Commission of the Reichstag: "We need no navy for coastal defence. Our coasts protect themselves." With the two naval bills an entirely new program was promulgated: on land and sea, Germany first! This marks the change from Bismarckian continental policies to "Welt-Politik," from the defensive to the offensive as the end and aim of Germany's military program. The language of these facts was so unmistakable that the Reichstag itself furnished the necessary commentary. Lieber, the leader of the Centrum at that time, spoke on the 11th of March, 1896, after a famous speech of the emperor on the occasion of the 25th anniversary of the founding of the German Empire, which had developed the new program as a forerunner to the naval bills, in which he mentioned "shoreless naval plans" against which Germany must be prepared to enter into active opposition. Another Centrum leader, Schadler, cried out in the Reichstag on March 23rd, 1898, when the first naval bill was under discussion, "The nation believes that we cannot be first on land and first on sea. You answer, gentlemen, that is not what we want! Nevertheless, gentlemen, you are at the beginning of such a conception, at a very strong beginning!" When the second bill came, the same Schadler declared in the Reischstag on the fifth of February, 1900, referring to previous promises that there would be no further naval bills, "and today comes this bill, which means nothing more and nothing less than the inauguration of a world fleet, as a basis of support for world policies, by doubling our navy and binding the next two decades by our demands." As a matter of fact the government openly defended the political program of its new course of action. On December 11th, 1899, Von Buelow, at that time state secretary of the foreign office, in a defence of the second naval bill stated, "when the English speak of 'a greater Britain,' when the French talk of 'la nouvelle France,' when the Russians open up Asia for themselves, we too have a right to aspire to a greater Germany. If we do not create a navy suffi- cient to protect our trade, our natives in foreign lands, our mis- sions and the safety of our shores, we are threatening the most vital interests of our nation. In the coming century the German people will be either the hammer or the anvil." Strip this of its coastal defence ornamentation, and there remains the colossal program: greater Germany, as the hammer upon other nations.

It is not difficult to determine the direction toward which these provocations, in the main, were directed. Germany was to become the rival of the world's great naval force—England. And England did not fail to understand. The naval reform bills, and the speeches that ushered them in, created a lively un- rest in England, an unrest that has never again subsided. In March, 1910, Lord Robert Cecil said in the House of Commons, during a naval debate: "I challenge any man to give me a plausible reason for the tremendous navy that Germany is build- ing up, other than to take up the fight against England." The fight for supremacy on the ocean that lasted for one and a half decades on both sides and culminated in the feverish building of dreadnoughts and super-dreadnoughts, was, in effect, the war between Germany and England. The naval bill of December 11, 1899, was a declaration of war by Germany, which England answered on August 4, 1914.

It should be noted that this fight for naval supremacy had nothing in common with the economic rivalry for the world market. The English "monopoly of the world market" which ostensibly hampered German industrial development, so much discussed at the present time, really belongs to the sphere of those war legends of which the ever green French "Revanche" is the most useful. This "monopoly" had become an old time fairy tale, to the lasting regret of the English capitalists. The industrial development of France, Belgium, Italy, Russia, India and Japan, and above all, of Germany and America, had put an end to this monopoly of the first half of the 19th century. Side by side with **England, one nation after** another stepped into the world market, capitalism developed automatically, and with gigantic strides, into world economy.

English supremacy on the sea, which has robbed so many social-democrats of their peaceful sleep, and which, it seems to these gentlemen, must be destroyed to preserve international socialism, had, up to this time, disturbed German capitalism so little that the latter was able to grow up into a lusty youth, with bursting cheeks, under its "yoke." Yes, England itself, and its colonies, were the cornerstone for German industrial growth. And similarly, Germany became, for the English nation, its most important and most necessary customer. Far from standing in each other's way, British and German capitalist development were mutually highly interdependent, and united by a far-reaching system of division of labor, strongly augmented by England's free trade policy. German trade and its interests in the world market, therefore, had nothing whatever to do with a change of front in German politics and with the building of its fleet.

Nor did German colonial possessions at that time come into conflict with the English control of the seas. German colonies were not in need of protection by a first-class sea power. No one, certainly not England, envied Germany her possessions. That they were taken during the war by England and Japan, that the booty had changed owners, is but a generally accepted war measure, just as German imperialist appetites clamor for Belgium, a desire that no man outside of an insane asylum would have dared to express in time of peace. Southeast and Southwest Africa, Wilhelmsland or Tsingtau would never have caused any war, by land or by sea, between Germany and England. In fact, just before the war broke out, a treaty regulating a peaceable division of the Portuguese colonies in Africa between these two nations had been practically completed.

When Germany unfolded its banner of naval power and world policies it announced the desire for new and far reaching conquest in the world by German imperialism. By means of a first class aggressive navy, and by military forces that increased in a parallel ratio, the apparatus for a future policy was established, opening wide the doors for unprecedented possibilities. Naval building and military armaments became the glorious business of German industry, opening up a boundless prospect for further operations by trust and bank capital in the whole wide world. Thus, the acquiescence of all capitalist parties and their rallying under the flag of imperialism was assured. The Centrum followed the example of the National Liberals, the staunchest defenders of the steel and iron industry, and, by adopting the naval bill it had loudly denounced in 1900, became the party of the government. The Progressives trotted after the Centrum when the successor to the naval bill—the high-tariff party—came up; while the Junkers, the staunchest opponents of the "horrid navy" and of the Canal, brought up the rear as the most enthusiastic porkers and parasites of the very policy of sea-militarism and colonial robbery they had so vehemently opposed. The Reichstag election of 1907, the so-called Hottentot Elections, found the whole of Germany in a paroxism of imperialistic enthusiasm, firmly united under one flag, that of the Germany of von Buelow, the Germany that felt itself ordained to play the role of the hammer in the world. These elections, with their spiritual progrom atmosphere, were a prelude to the Germany of August 4th, a challenge not only to the German working class, but to other capitalist nations as well, a challenge directed to no one in particular, a mailed fist shaken in the face of the entire world.

CHAPTER IV.

Turkey became the most important field of operations of German imperialism; the "Deutsche Bank," with its enormous Asiatic business interests, about which all German oriental policies center, became its pacemaker. In the 50's and 60's Asiatic Turkey worked chiefly with English capital, which built the railroad from Smyrna and leased the first stretch of the Anatolian railroad, up to Ismid. In 1888 German capital appeared upon the scene and procured from Abdul Hamid the control of the railroad that English capital had built and the franchise for the new stretch from Ismid to Angora and branch lines to Scutari, Brussa, Konia and Kaizarili. In 1899 the Deutsche Bânk secured concessions for the building and operation of a harbor and improvements in Hardar Pasha, and the sole control over trade and tariff collections in the harbor. In 1901 the Turkish Government turned over to the Deutsche Bank the concession for the great Bagdad railroad to the Persian Gulf, in 1907 for the drainage of the Sea of Karaviran and the irrigation of the Koma plain.

The reverse of this wonderful work of "peaceful culture" is the "peaceful" and wholesale ruin of the farming population of Asia Minor. The cost of this tremendous undertaking was advanced, of course, by the Deutsche Bank on the security of a widely diversified system of public indebtedness. Turkey will be, to all eternity, the debtor of Messrs. Siemens, Gwinner, Helfferich, etc., as it was formerly that of English, French and Austrian capital. This debtor, now, was forced not only to squeeze enormous sums out of the state to pay the interest on these loans, but, in addition, to guarantee a net income upon the railway thus built. The most modern methods of transportation were grafted upon a primitive, in many cases purely agricultural, population. From the unfruitful soil of farming sections that had been exploited unscrupulously, for years, by an oriental despotism, producing scarcely enough to feed the population after the huge state debts had been paid, it is practically impossible to secure the profits demanded by the railroads. Freight and traveling are exceedingly undeveloped, since the industrial and cultural character of the region is most primitive, and can improve only at a slow rate. The deficit that must be paid to raise the required profit is, therefore, paid by the Turkish Government in the form of a so-called kilometer guarantee. European Turkey was built up according to this system by Austrian and French capital, and the same system has been adopted by the Deutsche Bank in its operations in Asiatic Turkey. As bond and surety that the subsidy will be paid, the Turkish Government has handed over to the representatives of European capital, the so-called Executive Board in control of public debt, the main source of Turkish national income, which has given to the Deutsche Bank the right to collect the tithe from a number of provinces. In this way, for instance, the Turkish Government paid, from 1893 to 1910, for the railroad to Angora and for the line from Eskishehir to Konia, a subsidy of about 9,000,000 Frcs. The tithes thus leased by the Turkish Government to its European creditors are ancient payments rendered in produce such as corn, sheep, silk, etc. They are not collected directly but through sub-lessees, somewhat similar to the famous tax-collectors, so notorious in pre-revolutionary France, the state selling the right to raise the amount required from each vilayet (province) by auction, against cash payment. When the speculator or company has thus procured the right to collect the tithe of a vilayet, it, in turn, sells the tithe of each individual sanjak (district) to other speculators, who again divide their portion among a veritable band of smaller agents. Since each one of these collectors must not only cover his own expenses but secure as large a profit as possible besides, the tithe grows like a landslide as it approaches the farmer. If the lessee has been mistaken in his calculation, he seeks to recompense himself at the expense of the farmer. The latter, practically always in debt, waits impatiently for the time when he can sell his crop. But after his grain is cut he must frequently wait for weeks before the tithe collector comes to take his portion. The collector, who is usually graindealer as well, exploits this need of the farmer whose crop threatens to rot in the field, and persuades him to sell at a reduced price, knowing full well that it will be easy to secure the assistance of public officials and particularly of the muktar (town mayor) against the dissatisfied. When no tax-collector can be found the government itself collects the tithe in produce, puts it into storage houses and turns it over as part payment to the capitalists. This is the inner mechanism of the "industrial regeneration of Turkey" by European capital.

Thus a twofold purpose is accomplished. The farming population of Asia Minor becomes the object of a well organized process of exploitation in the interest of European, in this case German, financial and industrial capital. This again promotes the growth of the German sphere of interest in Turkey and lays the foundation for Turkey's "political protection." At the same time the instrument that carries out the exploitation of the farming population, the Turkish Government, becomes the willing tool and vassal of Germany's foreign policies. For many years Turkish finance, tariff policies, taxation and state expenditures have been under European control. German influence has made itself particularly felt in the Turkish military organization.

It is obvious from the foregoing, that the interests of German imperialism demand the protection of the Turkish State, to the extent at least of preventing its complete disintegration. The liquidation of Turkey would mean its division between England, Russia, Italy, and Greece among others and the basis for a large-scale operation by German capital would vanish. Moreover, an extraordinary increase in the power of Russia, England and the Mediterranean States would result. For German imperialism, therefore, the preservation of this accommodating apparatus of the "independent Turkish State," the "integrity" of Turkey is a matter of necessity. And this necessity will exist until such time as this state will fall, having been consumed from within by German capital, as was Egypt by England and more recently Morocco by France, into the lap of Germany. The well known spokesman of German imperialism, Paul Rohrbach, expressed this candidly and honestly when he said:

"In the very nature of things Turkey, surrounded on all sides by envious neighbors, must seek the support of a power that has practically no territorial interests in the Orient. That power is Germany. We, on the other hand, would be at a disadvantage if Turkey should disappear. If Russia and England fall heir to the Turkish State, obviously it will mean to both of these states a considerable increase in power. But even if Turkey should be so divided that we should also secure an extensive portion, it would mean for us endless difficulties. Russia, England, and in a certain sense France and Italy as well, are neighbors of present Turkish possessions and are in a position to hold and defend their portion by land and by sea. But we have no direct connection with the Orient. A German Asia Minor or Mesopotamia can become a reality only if Russia, and in consequence France as well, should be forced to relinquish their present political aims and ideals, i. e., if the world-war should take a decisive turn in favor of German interests."—(*The War and German Policy, page* 36).

Germany swore solemnly on November 8th, 1898, in Damascus, by the shadow of the great Saladin, to protect and to preserve the Mohammedan world and the green flag of the Prophet, and in so doing strengthened the regime of the bloody Sultan Abdul Hamid for over a decade. It has been able, after a short period of estrangement, to exert the same influence upon the Young Turk regime. Aside from conducting the profitable business of the Deutsche Bank, the German mission busied itself chiefly with the reorganization and training of Turkish militarism, under

German instructors with von der Goltz Pascha at the head. The modernization of the army, of course, piled new burdens upon the Turkish farmers, but it was a splendid business arrangement for Krupp and the Deutsche Bank. At the same time Turkish militarism became entirely dependent upon Prussian militarism, and became the centre of German ambitions in the Mediterranean and in Asia Minor.

That this "regeneration" of Turkey is a purely artificial attempt to galvanize a corpse, the fate of the Turkish revolutions best shows. In the first stage, while ideal considerations still predominated in the Young Turkish movement, when it was still fired with ambitious plans and illusions of a real springtime of life and of a rejuvenation for Turkey, its political sympathies were decidedly in favor of England. This country seemed to them to represent the ideal state of modern liberal rule, while Germany, which had so long played the role of protector of the holy regime of the old sultan was felt to be its natural opponent. For a while it seemed as if the revolution of 1908 would mean the bankruptcy of German oriental policies. It seemed certain that the overthrow of Abdul Hamid would go hand in hand with the downfall of German influence. As the Young Turks assumed power, however, and showed their complete inability to carry out any modern industrial, social or national reform on a large scale, as the counter-revolutionary hoof became more and more apparent, they turned of necessity to the tried and proven methods of Abdul Hamid, which meant periodic bloody massacres of oppressed peoples, goaded on until they flew at each other's throats, boundless, truly oriental exploitation of the farming population became the foundation of the nation. The artificial restoration of rule by force again became the most important consideration for "Young Turkey" and the traditional alliance of Abdul Hamid with Germany was reestablished as the deciding factor in the foreign policy of Turkey.

The multiplicity of national problems that threaten to dis-

rupt the Turkish nation make its regeneration a hopeless undertaking. The Armenian, Curdian, Syrian, Arabian, Greek, and
(up to the most recent times) the Albanian and Macedonian
questions, the manifold economic and social problems that exist
in the different parts of the realm, are a serious menace. The
growth of a strong, a hopeful, capitalism in the neighboring
Balkan states and the long years of destructive activity of international capital and international diplomacy stamp every attempt
to hold together this rotting pile of timber as nothing but a reactionary undertaking. This has long been apparent, particularly
to the German Social-Democracy. As early as 1896, at the
time of the Cretan uprising, the German Party press was filled
with long discussions on the Oriental problem, that led to a
revision of the attitude taken by Marx at the time of the Crimean
war and to the definite repudiation of the "integrity of Turkey"
as a heritage of European reaction. Nowhere was the Young
Turkish regime, its inner sterility and its counter-revolutionary
character, so quickly and so thoroughly recognized as in the German Social-Democratic press. It was a real Prussian idea, this
building of strategic railroads for rapid mobilization, this sending
of capable military instructors to prop up the crumbling edifice
of the Turkish State.

In 1912 the Young Turkish regiment was forced to abdicate
to the counter-revolution. Characteristically, the first act of
"Turkish regeneration" in this war was a coup d'état, the annihi-
lation of the constitution. In this respect too there was a formal
return to the rule of Abdul Hamid.

The first Balkan war brought bankruptcy to Turkish militarism, in spite of German training. And the present war, into
which Turkey was precipitated as Germany's "charge," will lead,
with inevitable fatality, to the further or to the final liquidation of the Turkish Empire.

The position of German militarism—and its essence, the interests of the Deutsche Bank—has brought the German Empire in

the Orient into opposition to all other nations. Above all to England. The latter had not only rival business relations and fat profits in Mesopotamia and Anatolia which were forced to retreat before their German rivals. This was a situation that English capitalism grudgingly accepted. But the building of strategic railroad, and the strengthening of Turkish militarism under German influence was felt by England to be a sore point, in a strategic question of its world political relations; lying as it did at the cross roads between Central Asia, Persia and India, on the one side, and Egypt on the other.

"England," writes Rohrbach in his *Bagdadbahn,* "can be attacked and mortally wounded on land in Egypt. The loss of Egypt will mean to England not only the loss of control over the Suez Canal and its connections with India and Asia, but probably the sacrifice of its possessions in Central and Eastern Africa as well. A Mohammedan power like Turkey, moreover, could exercise a dangerous influence over the 60 millions of Mohammedan subjects of England in India, in Afghanistan and Persia, should Turkey conquer Egypt. But Turkey can subjugate Egypt only if it possesses an extended system of railroads in Asia Minor and Syria, if by an extension of the Anatalion Railway it is able to ward off an English attack upon Mesopotamia, if it increases and improves its army, if its general economic and financial conditions are improved."

And in his *The War and German Policies,* which was published after the outbreak of the war, he says:

"The Bagdad Railroad was destined from the start to bring Constantinople and the military strongholds of the Turkish Empire in Asia Minor into direct connection with Syria and the provinces on the Euphrates and on the Tigris. Of course it was to be foreseen that this railway, together with the projected and, partly or wholly, completed railroads in Syria and Arabia, would make it possible to use Turkish troops in the direction of Egypt. No one will deny that, should the Turkish-German alliance remain in force, and under a number of other important conditions whose realization will be even more difficult than this alliance, the Bagdad Railway is a political life insurance policy for Germany."

Thus the semi-official spokesman of German imperialism openly revealed its plan and its aims in the Orient. Here German policies were clearly marked out, and an aggressive fundamental tendency most dangerous for the existing balance of world power, with a clearly defined point against England, was disclosed. German oriental policies became the concrete commentary to the naval policy inaugurated in 1899.

With its program for Turkish integrity, Germany came into conflict with the Balkan states, whose historic completion and inner growth are dependent upon the liquidation of European Turkey. It came into conflict with Italy, finally, whose imperialistic appetite was·likewise longing for Turkish possessions. At the Morocco Conference at Algeciras in 1905, Italy already sided with England and France. Six years later the Italian expedition to Tripolis, which followed the Austrian annexation of Bosnia and gave the signal for the Balkan War, already indicated a withdrawal of Italy, foreshadowed the disruption of the Triple Alliance and the isolation of German policies on this side as well. The other tendency of German expansionist desires in the west became evident in the Morocco affair. Nowhere was the negation of the Bismarck policy in Germany more clearly shown. Bismarck, as is well known, supported the colonial aspirations of France in order to distract its attention from Alsace-Lorraine. The new course of Germany, on the other hand, ran exactly counter to French colonial expansion. Conditions in Morocco were quite different from those that prevailed in Asiatic Turkey. Germany had few legitimate interests in Morocco. To be sure, German imperialists puffed up the claims of the German firm of Mannesmann, which had made a loan to the Moroccan sultan and demanded mining concessions in return, into a national issue.

But the well known fact that both of these rival groups in Morocco, the Mannesmann as well as the Krupp-Schneider Company are a thoroughly international mixture of German, French and Spanish capitalists, prevents anyone from seriously speaking of a German sphere of interest. The more symptomatic was the determination and the decisiveness with which the German Empire, in 1905, suddenly announced its claim to participation in the regulation of Moroccan affairs, and protested against French rule in Morocco. This was the first world-political clash with France. In 1895 Germany, together with France and Russia, assumed a threatening attitude toward victorious Japan to prevent it from exploiting its victory over China at Shimonoseki. Five years later it went arm in arm with France all along the line on a plundering expedition against China. Morocco caused a radical reorientation in Germany's relations with France. The Morocco crisis which, in the seven years of its duration, twice brought Europe to the verge of war between France and Germany, was not a question of "revenge" for continental conflicts between the two nations. An entirely new conflict had arisen, German imperialism had come into competition with that of France. In the end, Germany was satisfied with the French Congo region, and in accepting this admitted that it had no special interests to protect in Morocco itself. This very fact gave to the German attack in Morocco a far reaching political significance. The very indefinitiveness of its tangible aims and demands betrayed its insatiable appetite, the seeking and feeling for prey— it was a general imperialistic declaration of war against France. The contrast between the two nations here was brought into the limelight. On the one hand, a slow industrial development, a stagnant population, a nation living on its investments, concerned chiefly with foreign financial business, burdened with a large number of colonial possessions that it could hold together only with the utmost difficulty. On the other hand, a mighty young giant, a capitalism forging toward the first place among nations, going out into the world to hunt for colonies. English colonies were out of the question. So the hunger of German imperialism, besides feeding on Asiatic Turkey, turned at once to the French heritage. The French colonies moreover were a convenient bait with which Italy might eventually be attracted and repaid for Austrian desires of expansion on the Balkan peninsula, and be thus more firmly welded into the Triple Alliance by mutual business interests. The demands Germany made upon French imperialism were exceedingly disturbing, especially when it is remembered that Germany, once it had taken a foothold in any part of Morocco, could at any time set fire to the entire French North-African possessions, whose inhabitants were in a chronic state of incipient warfare with the French conquerors, by supplying them with ammunition. Germany's final withdrawal for suitable compensation did away with this immediate danger. But they could not allay the general disturbance in France and the world-political conflict that had been created.

Its Morocco policy not only brought Germany into conflict with France but with England as well. Here in Morocco, in the immediate neighborhood of Gibraltar, the second important center of world-political interests of the British Government, the sudden appearance of German imperialism with its demands, and the drastic impressiveness with which these demands were supported, were regarded as a demonstration against England as well. Furthermore the first formal protest of 1911 was directed specifically against the agreement of 1904 between England and France concerning Egypt and Morocco. Germany insisted briefly and definitely that England be disregarded in all further regulations of Moroccan affairs. The effect that such a demand was certain to have on German-English relations is obvious. The situation was commented upon in the *Frankfurter Zeitung* of November 8, 1911, by a London correspondent:

"This is the outcome: a million negroes in Congo, a great katzenjammer and a furious resentment against *perfides Albion*.

The katzenjammer Germany will live down. But what is to become of our relations with England? As they stand today matters are untenable. According to every historic probability they will either lead to something worse, that is war, or they will have to be speedily patched up. . . The trip of the Panther was, as a Berlin correspondent so well said in the *Frankfurter· Zeitung* the other day, a dig into the ribs of France to show that Germany is still here. . . Concerning the effect that this event would create here, Berlin cannot possibly entertain the slightest doubt. Certainly no correspondent in London was for a moment in doubt that England would stand energetically on the side of France. How can the *Norddeutsche Allgemeine Zeitung* still insist that Germany must treat with France alone? For several hundred years Europe has been the scene of a steadily increasing interweaving of political interests. The misfortune of one, according to the laws of politics, fills some with joy, others with apprehension. When two years ago Austria had its difficulties with Russia, Germany appeared upon the scene with shimmering armor, although Vienna, as was afterwards stated, would have preferred to settle matters without German intervention. It is very unlikely that England, having just emerged from a period of anti-German feeling, should consider that our dealings with France are none of its business. In the last analysis, it was a question of might; for a dig in the ribs, be it ever so friendly, is a very tangible matter. For no one can be quite sure when a blow on the teeth may follow. Since then the situation has become less critical. At the moment when Lloyd George spoke, the danger of a war between Germany and England was acute. Are we justified in expecting a different attitude from Sir Edward Grey after the policies that he and his followers have been pursuing? If Berlin entertained such ideas then it seems to me that the German foreign policies have been weighed and found wanting."

Thus·did our imperialistic policies create sharp conflicts in

Asia Minor and in Morocco, between England and Germany, between Germany and France. But what of German relations with Russia? In the murderous spirit that took possession of the German public during the first weeks of the war everything seemed credible. The German populace believed that Belgian women had gouged out the eyes of the German wounded, that Cossacks ate tallow candles, that they had taken infants by the legs and torn them to pieces; they believed that Russia aspired to the annexation of the German empire, to the destruction of German "Kultur," to the introduction of absolutism from Kiel to Munich, from the Warthe to the Rhine. The Social-Democratic *Chemnitzer Volksstimme* wrote on August 2nd:

"At this moment we all feel it our duty to fight first against the Russian knout. German women and children shall not become the victims of Russian bestiality, German territory must not fall into the hands of the cossacks. For if the Entente is victorious, not the French Republicans, but the Russian Tsar will rule over Germany. In this moment we defend everything that we possess of German culture and German freedom against a pitiless and barbarous foe."

On the same day the *Fraenkische Tagespost* cried out:

"Shall the cossacks, who have already taken possession of our border towns, in their onrush on our country, bring destruction to our cities? Shall the Russian Czar, whose love of peace the Social-Democrats refused to trust even on the day when his peace manifesto was published, who is the worst enemy of the Russian people themselves, rule over one man of German blood?"

And the *Koenigsberger Volkszeitung* wrote on August 3rd:

"Not one of us can doubt, whether he is liable for military service or not, that he must do everything to keep these worthless vandals from our borders so long as the war may last. For if they should be victorious, thousands of our comrades will be condemned to horrible prison sentences. Under the Russian scepter there is no such thing as self-expression of the people, no social-democratic press is allowed to exist, social-democratic meetings and organizations are prohibited. We cannot conceive for a moment the possibility of a Russian victory. While still upholding our opposition to war, we will all work together to protect ourselves against these vandals that rule the Russian nation."

We shall later enter a little more fully into the relations that exist between German culture and Russian Czarism. They form a chapter by itself in the position of the German Social-Democracy on the war. This much may be said now, one might with as much justification assume that the Czar desires to annex Europe, or the moon, as to speak of his desire to annex Germany. In the present war only two nations are threatened in their national existence, Belgium and Servia. While we howled about safeguarding the national existence of Germany, our cannon were directed against these two states. It is impossible to discuss with people who still believe in the possibility of ritual murder. But to those who do not act from mob instinct, who do not think in terms of clumsy slogans that are invented to catch the rabble, who guide their thoughts by historic facts, it must be obvious that Russian Czarism cannot have such intentions. Russia is ruled by desperate criminals, but not by maniacs. And after all, the policies of absolutism, in spite of all their characteristic differences, have this similarity in all nations, that they live not on thin air but upon very real possibilities, in a realm where concrete things come into the closest contact with each other. We need have no fear of the arrest of our German comrades and their banishment to Siberia, nor of the introduction of Russian absolutism into Germany. For the statesmen of the bloody Czar, with all their mental inferiority, have a clearer materialistic conception of the situation than some of our party editors. These statesmen know very well that political forms of government cannot be "introduced" anywhere and everywhere according to the desire of the rulers; they know full well that every form of government is the outcome of certain economic and social foundations, they know from bitter experience that even in Russia itself conditions are almost beyond their power to control; they know, finally, that reaction in every country can use only the forms that are in accord with the nature of the country, and that the absolutism that is in accord with our class and party conditions is the Hohenzollern police state and the Prussian three-class electoral system. A dispassionate consideration of the whole situation will show that we need not fear that Russian Czarism, even if it should win a complete victory over Germany, would feel called upon to do away with these products of German culture.

In reality the conflicts that exist between Germany and Russia are of an entirely different nature. These differences are not to be found in the field of inner politics. Quite the contrary: their mutual tendencies and internal relationships have established a century-old traditional friendship between the two nations. But in spite of and notwithstanding their solidarity on questions of inner policy, they have come to blows in the field of foreign, world-political hunting grounds.

Russian imperialism, like that of western nations, consists of widely diversified elements. Its strongest strain is not, however, as in Germany or England, the economic expansion of capital, hungry for territorial accumulation, but the political interests of the nation. To be sure, Russian industry can show a considerable export to the Orient, to China, Persia and Central Asia, and the Czarist Government seeks to encourage this export trade because it furnishes a desirable foundation for its sphere of interest. But national policies here play an active, not a passive, role. On the one hand, the traditional tendencies of a conquest-loving Czardom, ruling over a mighty nation whose population today consists of 172 millions of human beings, demand free access to the ocean, to the Pacific Ocean on the East, to the Mediterranean on the South, for industrial as well as for strategic reasons. On the other hand, the very existence of absolutism, and the necessity of holding a respected place in the world-political field, and finally the need of financial credit in foreign countries, without which Czarism cannot exist, all play their important part. We must add to these, as in every other monarchy, the dynastic interest. Foreign prestige and temporary forgetfulness of inner problems and difficulties are well known family remedies in the art of ruling, when a conflict arises between the government and the great mass of the people.

But modern capitalist interests are becoming more and more a factor in the imperialist aims of the Czarist nation. Russian capitalism, still in its earliest youth, cannot hope to perfect its development under an absolutist regime. On the whole it has advanced little beyond the primitive stage of home industry. But it sees a gigantic future before its eyes in the exploitation of the nation's natural resources. As soon as Russia's absolutism is swept away, of this there can be no doubt, Russia will develop rapidly into the foremost capitalist nation, provided always that the international situation will give it the time necessary for such development. It is this hope, and the appetite for foreign markets that will mean increased capitalistic development even at the present time, that has filled the Russian bourgeoisie with imperialistic desires and led them to eagerly voice their demands in the coming division of the world's resources. This historic desire is actively supported by very tangible immediate interests. There are, in the first place, the armament industry and its purveyors. In the second place the conflicts with the "enemy within," the revolutionary proletariat, have given to the Russian bourgeoisie an increased appreciation of the powers of militarism and the distracting effects of a world-political evangel. It has bound together the various capitalist groups and the nobility under one counter-revolutionary regime. The imperialism of bourgeois Russia, particularly among the Liberals, has grown enormously in the stormy atmosphere of the revolutionary period, and has given to the traditional foreign policies of the Romanoffs a modern stamp. Chief among the aims of the traditional policies of monarchic Russia, as well as of the more modern appetites of the Russian bourgeoisie, are the Dardanelles. They are, according to the famous remark made by Bismarck, the latchkey to the Russian possessions on the Black Sea. Since the eighteenth century, Russia has waged a number of bloody wars against Turkey, has undertaken its mission as the liberator of the Balkans, for the realization of this goal. For this ideal, Russia has piled up mountains of dead in Ismael, in Navarin, in Sinope, Silistria and Sebastopol, in Plevna and Shipka. To the Russian muzhik, the defense of his Slavic and Christian brothers from the horrors of Turkish oppression has become as potent a war legend as the defense of German culture and freedom against the horrors of Russia has become to the German Social-Democracy.

But the Russian bourgeoisie also was much more enthusiastic over the Mediterranean prospect than for its Manchurian and Mongolian "mission." The liberal bourgeoisie of Russia criticised the Japanese war so severely as a senseless adventure, because it distracted the attention of Russian politics from the problem that was to them more important, the Balkans. And in another way, the unfortunate war with Japan had the same effect. The extension of Russian power into Eastern and Central Asia, to Thibet and down into Persia necessarily aroused a feeling of discomfort in the minds of English imperialists. England, fearing for its enormous Indian empire, viewed the Asiatic movements of Russia with growing suspicion. In fact, at the beginning of the present century the English-Russian conflict in Asia was the strongest world-conflict in the international situation. Moreover this will be, in all probability, the most critical issue in future world-political developments when the present war is over. The crushing defeat of Russia in 1904 and the subsequent outbreak of the Russian revolution only temporarily changed the situation. The apparent weakening of the empire of the Czar brought about a relaxation of the tension between England and Russia. In 1907 a treaty was signed between the two nations providing for a mutual control of Persia that established, for the time being, friendly and neighborly relations in Central Asia. This kept Russia from undertaking great projects in the East, and her energies reverted all the more vigorously to their old occupation, Balkan politics. Here the Russia of the Czar came for the first time into sharp conflict with German culture, after a century of faithful and well-founded friendship. The road to the Dardanelles leads over the corpse of Turkey. But for more than a decade Germany has regarded the "integrity" of this corpse as its most important world-political task. Russian methods in the Balkans had changed at various times. Embittered by the ingratitude of the liberated Balkan Slavs who tried to escape from their position as vassals to the Czarist Government, Russia for a time supported the program of Turkish integrity with the silent understanding that the division of that country should be postponed to some more auspicious time. But today the final liquidation of Turkey coincides with the plans of both Russian and English politics. The latter aims to unite Arabia and Mesopotamia, and the Russian territories that lie between Egypt and India, under British rule, into a great Mohammedan empire, thus conserving its own position in India and Egypt. In this way Russian imperialism, as in earlier times English imperialism, came into opposition with that of Germany. For this privileged exploiter of Turkish disintegration had taken up her position as sentinel on the Bosphorus.

Russian interests came to a clash in the Balkans not only directly with Germany but with Austria as well. Austrian imperialism is the political complement of German imperialism, at the same time its Siamese twin brother and its fate.

Germany, having isolated herself on all sides by her world policy, has in Austria her only ally. The alliance with Austria is old, having been founded by Bismarck in 1879. But since that time it has completely changed its character. Like the enmity toward France, the alliance with Austria received an entirely new content through the development of the last decades. In 1879 its chief purpose was the mutual defense of the possessions gained in the wars of 1864-1870. The Bismarck Triple Alliance was conservative in character, especially since it signified Austria's final renunciation of admission to the German federation of states, its acceptance of the state of affairs created by Bismarck, and the military hegemony of Greater Prussia. The Balkan aspirations of Austria were as distasteful to Bismarck as the South-African conquests of Germany. In his *Gedanken und Erinnerungen* he says:

"It is natural that the inhabitants of the Danube region should have needs and aspirations that extend beyond the present boundaries of their monarchy. The German national constitution points out the way along which Austria can form a union of the political and material interests that exist between the most eastern Rumanian tribe and the Bay of Cattaro. But the duty of the German Empire does not demand that it satisfy the desires of its neighbors for increased territory with the blood and wealth of its subjects."

He expressed the same thought still more drastically when he uttered the well known sentiment that, to him, the whole of Bosnia was not worth the bone of a Pomeranian grenadier. Indeed, a treaty drawn up with Russia in 1884 proves conclusively that Bismarck never desired to place the Triple Alliance at the service of Austrian annexationist desires. By this treaty, the German Empire promised, in the event of a war between Austria and Russia, not to support the former, but rather to observe a "benevolent neutrality."

But since imperialism has taken hold of German politics, its relations to Austria have changed as well. Austria-Hungary lies between Germany and the Balkan, in other words, on the road over the critical point in German Oriental politics. To make Austria its enemy at this time would mean complete isolation, and complete abdication by Germany of its world-political plan.

But the weakening of Austria, which would signify the final liquidation of Turkey, with a consequent strengthening of Russia,
the Balkan States, and England, would probably accomplish the
national unification of Germany, but would, at the same time,
wipe out, forever, its imperialistic aspirations. The safety of the
Hapsburg monarchy has therefore logically become a necessary
complement to German imperialism, the preservation of Turkey
its chief problem.

But Austria means a constant latent state of war in the Balkans. For Turkish disintegration has promoted the existence and
growth of the Balkan States in the immediate neighborhood of
the Hapsburg monarchy, and the resulting state of chronic incipient warfare. Obviously the existence of virile and independent national states on the border of a monarchy that is made
up of fragments of these same nationalities, which it can rule
only by the whip-lash of dictatorship must hasten its downfall.
Austrian Balkan politics and particularly its Serbian relations
have plainly revealed its inner decay. Although its imperialistic
appetites wavered between Saloniki and Durazzo, Austria was
not in a position to annex Servia, even before the latter had
grown in strength and size through the two Balkan wars. For
the forcible annexation of Servia would have dangerously
strengthened in its interior one of the most refractory South
Slavic nationalities, a people that even now, because of Austria's
stupid regime of reaction, can scarcely be held in check. But
neither can Austria tolerate the normal independent development
of Servia or profit from it by normal commercial relations. For
the Habsburg monarchy is not the political expression of a capitalist state, but a loose syndicate of a few parasitic cliques, striv-
ing to grasp everything within reach, utilizing the political powers
of the nation so long as this weak edifice still stands. For the
benefit of Hungarian agrarians, and for the purpose of increasing the prices of agricultural products, Austria has forbidden

Servia to send cattle and fruits into Austria, thus depriving this nation of farmers of its most important market. In the interests of Austrian monopolies it has forced Servia to import industrial products exclusively from Austria, and at the highest prices. To keep Servia in a state of economic and political dependence, it prevented Servia from uniting on the East with Bulgaria, to secure access to the Black Sea, and from securing access to the Adriatic, on the West, by prohibiting the acquisition of a harbor in Albania. In short, the Balkan policy of Austria was nothing more than a barefaced attempt to choke off Servia. Also, it was directed against the establishment of mutual relations between, and against the inner growth of the Balkan States, and was, therefore, a constant menace for them.

Austrian imperialism constantly threatened the existence and development of the Balkan States; now by the annexation of Bosnia, now by its demands upon the Sanjak of Novibazar and on Saloniki, now by its encroachments upon the Albanian coast. To satisfy these tendencies on the part of Austria, and to meet the competition of Italy as well, the caricature of an independent Albania under the rule of a German nobleman was created after the second Balkan war, a country which was, from the first hour, little more than the plaything of the intrigues of imperialistic rivals.

Thus the imperialistic policies of Austria during the last decade were a constant hindrance to the normal progressive development of the Balkans, and led to the inevitable alternative: either the Habsburg monarchy or the capitalist development of the Balkan States.

Emancipated from Turkish rule, the Balkan now faced its new hindrance, Austria, and the necessity of removing it from its path. Historically the liquidation of Austria-Hungary is the logical sequence of Turkish disintegration, and both are in direct line with the process of historical development.

There was but one solution: war—a world war. For behind Servia stood Russia, unable to sacrifice its influence in the Balkans and its role of "protector" without giving up its whole imperialisitc program in the Orient as well. In direct conflict with Austrian politics, Russia aimed to unite the Balkan States under a Russian protectorate, to be sure. The Balkan union that had almost completely annihilated European Turkey in the victorious war of 1912 was the work of Russia, and was directly and intentionally aimed against Austria. Inspite of Russian efforts, the Balkan union was smashed in the second Balkan war. But Servia, emerging the victor, became dependent upon the friendship of Russia in the same degree as Austria had become Russia's bitter enemy. Germany, whose fate was firmly linked to that of the Habsburg monarchy, was obliged to back up the stupid Balkan policy of the latter, step by step, and was thus brought into a doubly aggravated opposition to Russia.

But the Balkan policies of Austria, furthermore, brought Austria into conflict with Italy, which was actively interested in the dissolution of the Turkish and Austrian Empires. The imperialism of Italy has found in the Italian possessions of Austria a most popular cloak for its own annexationist desires. Its eyes are directed especially toward the Albanian coast of the Adriatic, should a new regulation of Balkan affairs take place. The Triple Alliance, having already sustained a severe blow in the Tripolitan war, was destroyed by the acute crisis in the Balkans during the two Balkan wars. The Central Powers were thus brought into conflict with the entire outside world. German imperialism, chained to two decaying corpses, was steering its course directly toward a world war.

Moreover, Germany embarked upon this course with a full realization of its consequences. Austria, as the motive power, was rushing blindly into destruction. Its clique of clerical-militarist rulers with the Archduke Franz Ferdinand and his right hand man Baron von Chlumezki at the head, fairly jumped at every excuse to strike the first blow. In 1909 Austria framed up the famous documents by Professor Friedmann, exposing what purported to be a widespread, criminal conspiracy of the Serbs against the Habsburg monarchy, for the sole purpose of infusing the German nations with the necessary war-enthusiasm. These papers had only one slight drawback—they were forged from beginning to end. A year later the rumor of the horrible martyrdom of the Austrian consul Prohaska in Ueskub was busily spread for days to serve as the spark that would ignite the keg of powder, while Prohaska roamed unmolested and happy through the streets of Ueskub. Then came the assassination at Serajewo, a long desired, truly shameful crime. "If ever a blood sacrifice has had a liberating, releasing effect, it was the case here," rejoiced the spokesman of German imperialism. Among Austrian imperialists the rejoicing was still greater, and they decided to use the noble corpses while they were still warm. After a hurried conference with Berlin, war was virtually decided and the ultimatum sent out as a flaming torch that was to set fire to the capitalist world at all four corners.

But the occurrence at Serajewo only furnished the immediate pretext. Causes and conflicts for the war had been overripe for a long time. The conjuncture that we witness today was ready a decade ago. Every year, every political occurrence of recent years has but served to bring war a step nearer: the Turkish revolution, the annexation of Bosnia, the Morocco crisis, the Tripolis expedition, the two Balkan wars. All military bills of the last years were drawn up in direct preparation for this war; the countries of Europe were preparing, with open eyes, for the inevitable final contest. Five times during recent years this war was on the verge of an outbreak: in the summer of 1905, when Germany for the first time made her decisive demands in the Morocco crisis; in the summer of 1908, when England, Russia and France threatened with war after the conference of the monarchs in Reval over the Macedonian question, and war was prevented only by the sudden outbreak of the Turkish revolution; in the beginning of 1909 when Russia replied to the Bosnian annexation with a mobilization, when Germany in Petersburg formally declared its readiness to go to war on the side of Austria; in the summer of 1911 when the "Panther" was sent to Agadir, an act that would certainly have brought on war if Germany had not finally acquiesced in the Morocco question and allowed itself to be compensated with the Congo concession; and finally, in the beginning of 1913, when Germany, in view of the proposed Russian invasion of Albania, a second time threatened Petersburg with its readiness for warlike measures.

Thus the world war has been hanging fire for eight years. It was postponed again and again only because always one of the two sides in question was not yet ready with its military preparations.

So, for instance, the present world war was imminent at the time of the "Panther" adventure in 1911—without a murdered Grand Duke, without French fliers over Nuremberg, without a Russian invasion into East Prussia. Germany simply put it off for a more favorable moment—one need only read the frank explanation of a German imperialist: "The German government has been accused by the so-called pan-Germans of weakness in the Morocco crisis in 1911." Let them disabuse their minds of this false impression. It is a fact that, at the time when we sent the "Panther" to Agadir, the reconstruction of the North-East Sea Canal was still in progress, that building operations on Helgoland for the construction of a great fort were nowhere near completion, that our fleet of dreadnoughts and accessories, in comparison with the English sea power, was in a far more unfavorable position than was the case three years later.

Compared to the present time, 1914, the canal as well as Helgoland were in a deplorable state of unreadiness, were partially absolutely useless for war purposes. Under such circumstances, where one knows that one's chances will be far more favorable in a few years, it would be worse than foolish to provoke a war. First the German fleet had to be put in order; the great military bill had to be pushed through the Reichstag. In the summer of 1914 Germany was prepared for war, while France was still laboring over its three years military service program, while in Russia neither the army nor the naval program were ready. It was up to Germany to utilize the auspicious moment."

The same Rohrbach, who is not only the most serious representative of imperialism in Germany, but is also in intimate touch with the leading circles in German politics and is their semi-official mouthpiece, comments upon the situation in July, 1914, as follows. "At this time there was only one danger, that we might be morally forced, by an apparent acquiescence on the part of Russia, to wait until Russia and France were really prepared." In other words, Germany feared nothing so much as that Russia might give in. "With deep pain we saw our untiring efforts to preserve world peace shipwrecked, etc., etc."

The invasion of Belgium, therefore, and the accomplished fact of war was not a bolt from the blue. It did not create a new, unheard of situation. Nor was it an event that came, in its political associations, as a complete surprise to the social-democratic group. The world war that began officially on August 4th, 1914, was the same world war toward which German imperialism had been driving for decades, the same war whose coming the Social-Democracy had prophesied year after year. This same war has been denounced by social-democratic parliamentarians, newspapers and leaflets a thousand times as a frivolous imperialistic crime, as a war that is against every interest of culture and against every interest of the nation.

And, indeed, not the "existence and the independent develop-

ment of Germany in this war" are at stake, in spite of he reitera
tions of the social-democratic press, but the immediate profits of
the "Deutsche Bank" in Asiatic Turkey and the future profits of
the "Mannesmann" and "Krupp" interests in Morocco, the existence and the reactionary character of Austria, "this heap of organized decay, that calls itself the Habsburg monarchy," as the
"Vorwaerts" wrote on the 25th of July, 1914; Hungarian pigs
and prunes, paragraph 14, the "Kultur" of Friedmann-Prohaska,
the existence of Turkish rule in Asia Minor and of counter-revolution on the Balkan.

Our party press was filled with moral indignation over the fact
that Germany's foes should drive black men and barbarians, Negroes, Sikhs and Maoris into the war. Yet these peoples play a
role in this war that is approximately identical with that played
by the socialist proletariat in the European states. If the Maoris
of New Zealand were eager to risk their skulls for the English
king, they showed only as much understanding of their own interests as the German Social-Democratic group that traded the
existence, the freedom and the civilization of the German people
for the existence of the Habsburg monarchy, for Turkey and for
the vaults of the "Deutsche Bank."

One difference there is between the two. A generation ago,
Maori negroes were still cannibals and not students of Marxian
philosophy.

CHAPTER V.

But Czarism! In the first moments of the war this was undoubtedly the factor that decided the position of our party. In its declaration, the social-democratic group had given the slogan: Against Czarism! And out of this the socialist press has made a fight for European culture.

The *Frankfurter Volksstimme* wrote on July 31:

"The German Social-Democracy has always hated Czardom as the bloody guardian of European reaction: From the time that Marx and Engels followed, with far-seeing eyes, every movement of this barbarian government, down to the present day, where its prisons are filled with political prisoners, and yet it trembles before every labor movement. The time has come when we must square accounts with these terrible scoundrels, under the German flag of war."

The *Pfaelzische Post* of Ludwighafen wrote on the same day:

"This is a principle that was first established by our August Bebel. This is the struggle of civilization against barbarism, and in this struggle the proletariat will do its share."

The *Muenchener Post* of August 1st:

"When it comes to defending our country against the bloody Czardom we will not be made citizens of the second class."

The *Halle Volksblatt* wrote on August 5th:

"If this is so, if we have been attacked by Russia, and everything seems to corroborate this statement—then the Social-Democracy, as a matter of course, must vote in favor of all means of defense. With all our strength we must fight to drive Czarism from our country!"

And on August 18th:

"Now that the die is cast in favor of the sword, it is not only the duty of national defense and national existence that puts the weapon into our hands as into the hands of every German, but also the realization that in the enemy whom we are fighting in the east we are striking a blow at the foe of all culture and all progress. . . . The overthrow of Russia is synonymous with the victory of freedom in Europe. . . "

On August 5th, the *Braunschweiger Volksfreund* wrote:

"The irresistible force of military preparation drives everything before it. But the class-conscious labor movement obeys, not an outside force, but its own conviction, when it defends the ground upon which it stands, from attack in the east."

The *Essener Arbeiterzeitung* cried out on August 3rd:

"If this country is threatened by Russia's determination, then the Social-Democrats, since the fight is against Russian Blood-Czarism, against the perpetrator of a million crimes against freedom and culture, will allow none to excell them in the fulfilment of their duty, in their willingness to sacrifice. Down with Czarism! Down with the home of Barbarism! Let that be our slogan!"

Similarly the *Bielefelder Volkswacht* writes on August 4th:

"Everywhere the same cry: against Russian Despotism and faithlessness."

The Elberfeld party-organ on August 5th:

"All western Europe is vitally interested in the extermination of rotten murderous Czarism. But this human interest is crushed by the greed of England and France to check the profits that have been made possible by German capital."

The *Rheinische Zeitung* in Cologne:

"Do your duty, friends, wherever fate may place you. You are fighting for the civilization of Europe, for the independence of your fatherland, for your own welfare."

The *Schleswig-Holstein Volkszeitung* of August 7th writes:

"Of course we are living in an age of capitalism. Of course we will continue to have class struggles after the great war is over. But these class struggles will be fought out in a freer state, they will be far more confined to the economic field than before. In the future the treatment of Socialists as outcasts, as citizens of the second class, as politically rightless will be impossible, once the Czardom of Russia has vanished."

On August 11th, the *Hamburger Echo* cried:

"We are fighting to defend ourselves not so much against England and France as against Czarism. But this war we carry on with the greatest enthusiasm, for it is the war for civilization."

And the Luebeck party-organ declared, as late as September 4th:

"If European liberty is saved, then Europe will have German arms to thank for it. Our fight is a fight against the worst enemy of all liberty and all democracy."

Thus the chorus of the German party press sounded and resounded.

In the beginning of the war the German government accepted the proffered assistance. Nonchalantly it fastened the laurels of the liberator of European culture to its helmet. Yes, it endeavored to carry through the role of the "liberator of nations," though often with visible discomfort and rather awkward grace. It flattered the Poles and the Jews in Russia, and egged one nation on against the other, using the policies that had proven so successful in their colonial warfare, where again and again they played up one chief against the other. And the Social-Democrats followed each leap and bound of German imperialism with remarkable agility. While the Reichstag group covered up every shameful outrage with a discrete silence the social-democratic press filled the air with jubilant melodies, rejoicing in the liberty that "German riflebutts" had brought to the poor victims of Czarism.

Even the theoretical organ of the party, the *Neue Zeit,* wrote on the 28th of August:

"The border population of the "little father's" realm greeted the coming of the German troops with cries of joy. For these Poles and Jews have but one conception of their fatherland, that of corruption and rule by the knout. Poor devils, really father-landless creatures, these downtrodden subjects of bloody Nicholas. Even should they desire to do so, they could find nothing to defend but their chains. And so they live and toil, hoping and longing that German rifles, carried by German men, will crush the whole Czarist system. . . . A clear and definite purpose still lives in the German working-class, though the thunder of a world-war is crashing over its head. It will defend itself from the allies of Russian barbarism in the west to bring about an honorable peace. It will give to the task of destroying Czarism the last breath of man and beast."

After the social-democratic group had stamped the war as a war of defense for the German nation and European culture, the social-democratic press proceeded to hail it as the "savior of the oppressed nations." Hindenburg became the executor of Marx and Engels.

The memory of our party has played it a shabby trick. It forgot all its principles, its pledges, the decision of international congresses just at the moment when they should have found their application. And to its great misfortune, it remembered the heritage of Karl Marx and dug it out of the dust of passing years at the very moment when it could serve only to decorate Prussian militarism, for whose destruction Karl Marx was willing to sacrifice "the last breath of man and beast." Long forgotten chords that were sounded by Marx in the *Neue Rheinische Zeitung* against the vassal state of Nicholas I, during the German March Revolution of 1848, suddenly reawakened in the ears of the German Social-Democracy in the year of Our Lord

1914, and called them to arms, arm in arm with Prussian junkerdom against the Russia of the Great Revolution of 1905.

This is where a revision should have been made; the s'ogans
of the March Revolution should have been brought into accord
with the historical experiences of the last seventy years.

In 1848 Russia Czarism was, in truth, "the guardian of European reaction." The product of Russian social conditions, firmly
rooted in its medieval, agricultural state, absolutism was the
protector and at the same time the mighty director of monarchical reaction. This was weakened, particularly in Germany,
where a system of small states still obtained. As late as 1851 it
was possible for Nicholas I, to assure Berlin through the Prussian consul von Rochow "that he would, indeed, have been pleased
to see the revolution destroyed to the roots when general von
Wrangel advanced upon Berlin in November, 1848." At another
time, in a warning to Manteuffel; the Czar stated, "that he relied
upon the Imperial Ministry, under the leadership of His High-
ness, to defend the rights of the crown against the chambers,
and give to the principles of conservatism their due." It was
possible for the same Nicholas I to bestow the Alexander Nevski
order on a Prussian Ministerial President in recognition of his
"constant efforts . . . to maintain legal order in Prussia."

The Crimean war worked a noticeable change in this respect.
It ended with the military and therefore with the political bankruptcy of the old system. Russian absolutism was forced to
grant reforms, to modernize its rule, to adjust itself to capitalist
conditions. In so doing, it gave its little finger to the devil who
already holds it firmly by the arm, and will eventually get it altogether. The Crimean War was, by the way, an instructive example of the kind of liberation that can be brought to a downtrodden people "at the point of the gun." The military overthrow at
Sedan brought France its republic. But this republic was not the

gift of the Bismarck soldiery. Prussia at that time, as today, can give to other peoples nothing but its own junker rule. The republican France was the ripe fruit of inner social struggles and of the three revolutions that had preceded it. The crash at Sebastopol was in effect similar to that of Jena. But because there was no revolutionary movement in Russia, it led to the outward renovation and reaffirmation of the old regime.

But the reforms that opened the road for capitalist development in Russia during the 60's were possible only with the money of a capitalist system. This money was furnished by western European capital. It came from Germany and France, and has created a new relationship that has lasted down to the present day. Russian absolutism is now subsidized by the western European bourgeoisie. No longer does the Russian Ruble "roll in diplomatic chambers" as Prince William of Prussia bitterly complained in 1854, "into the very chambers of the King." On the contrary, German and French money is rolling to Petersburg to feed a regime that would long ago have breathed its last without this life-giving juice. Russian Czarism is today no longer the product of Russian conditions; its root lies in the capitalist conditions of western Europe. And the relationship is shifting from decate to decade. In the same measure as the old root of Russian absolutism in Russia itself is being destroyed, the new, west-European root is growing stronger and stronger. Besides lending their financial support, Germany and France, since 1870, have been vieing with each other to lend Russia their political support as well. As revolutionary forces arise from the womb of the Russian people itself to fight against Russian absolutism, they meet with an ever growing resistence in western Europe, which stands ready to lend to threatened Czarism its moral and political support. So when, in the beginning of the 80's the older Russian socialist movement severely shook the Czarist government and partly destroyed its authority within and without, Bis-

marck made his treaty with Russia and strengthened its position
in international politics.

Capitalist development, tenderly nurtured by Czarism with its
own hands, finally bore fruit: in the 90's the revolutionary movement of the Russian proletariat began. The erstwhile "guardian of reaction" was forced to grant a meaningsless constitution,
to seek a new protector from the rising flood in its own country.
And it found this protector—in Germany. The Germany of Buelow must pay the debt of gratitude that the Prussia of Wrangel
and Manteuffel had incurred. Relations were completely reversed.
Russian support against the revolution in Germany is superseded
by German aid against the revolution in Russia. Spies, outrages,
betrayals—a demagogic agitation, like that which blessed the
times of the Holy Alliance, was unleashed in Germany against
the fighters for the cause of Russian freedom, and followed them
to the very doorsteps of the Russian Revolution. In the Koenigsberg trial of 1904 this wave of persecution was at its height. This
trial threw a scathing light upon a whole historical development
since 1848 and showed the complete change of relations between
Russian absolutism and European reaction. *"Tua res agitur!"*
cried a Prussian Minister of Justice to the ruling classes of Germany, pointing to the tottering foundation of the Czarist regime.
"The establishment of a democratic republic in Russia would
strongly influence Germany," declared First District-Attorney
Schulze in Koenigsberg. "When my neighbor's home burns my
own is also in danger." And his assistant Casper also emphasized: "it is naturally not indifferent to Germany's public interests
whether this bulwark of absolutism stands or falls. Certainly the
flames of a revolutionary movement may easily spring over into
Germany. . ."

The Revolution was overthrown, but the very causes that led
to its temporary downfall are valuable in a discussion of the position taken by the German Social-Democracy in this war. That

the Russian uprising in 1905-1906 was unsuccessful inspite of its unequalled expenditure of revolutionary force, its clearness of purpose and tenacity, can be ascribed to two distinct causes. The one lies in the inner character of the Revolution itself, in its enormous historical program, in the mass of economic and political problems that it was forced to face. Some of them, for instance, the agrarian problem, cannot possibly be solved within capitalist society. There was the difficulty, furthermore, of creating a class-state for the supremacy of the modern bourgeoisie against the counter-revolutionary opposition of the bourgeoisie as a whole. To the onlooker it would seem that the Russian Revolution was doomed to failure because it was a proletarian revolution with bourgeois duties and problems, or if you wish, a bourgeois revolution waged by socialist proletarian methods, a crash of two generations amid lightning and thunder, the fruit of the delayed industrial development of class conditions in Russia and their overripeness in western Europe. From this point of view its downfall in 1906 signifies not its bankruptcy, but the natural closing of the first chapter, upon which the second must follow with the inevitability of a natural law. The second cause was of external nature: it lay in western Europe: European reaction once more hastened to help its endangered protégé. Not with lead and bullets, although "German guns" were in German fists even in 1905 and only waited for a signal from Petersburg to attack the neighboring Poles. Europe rendered an assistance that was equally valuable: financial subsidy and political alliances were arranged to help Czarism in Russia. French money paid for the armed forces that broke down the Russian Revolution; from Germany came moral and political support that helped the Russian government to clamber out from the depths of shame into which Japanese torpedoes and Russian proletarian fists had thrust it. In 1910, in Potsdam, official Germany received Russian Czarism with open arms. The reception of the bloodstained monarch at the gates of the German capital was not only the German blessing for the throttling of Persia, but above all for the hangman's work of the Russian counter-revolution. It was the official banquet of German and Europeon Kultur over what they believed to be the grave of the Russian Revolution.

And strange! At that time, when this challenging feast upon the grave of the Russian Revolution was held in its own home, the German Social-Democracy remained silent, and had completely forgotten "the heritage of our masters" from 1848. At that time, when the hangman was received in Potsdam, not a sound, not a protest, not an article vetoed this expression of solidarity with the Russian counter-revolution. Only since this war has begun, since the police permits it, the smallest party organ intoxicates itself with bloodthirsty attacks upon the hangman of Russian liberty. Yet nothing could have disclosed more clearly than did this triumphal tour of the Czar in 1910, that the oppressed Russian proletariat was the victim not only of domestic reaction but of western European reaction as well. Their fight, like that of the March revolutionists in 1848, was against reaction, not only in their own country, but against its guardians in all other European countries.

After the inhuman crusades of the counter-revolution had somewhat subsided, the revolutionary ferment in the Russian proletariat once more became active. The flood began to rise and to boil. Economic strikes in Russia, according to the official reports, involved 46,623 workers and 256,386 days in 1910; 96,730 workers and 768,556 days in 1911; and 89,771 workers and 1,214,881 days in the first five months of 1912. Political mass-strikes, protests and demonstrations comprised 1,005,000 workers in 1912, 1,272,000 in 1913. In 1914 the flood rose higher and higher. On January 22nd, the anniversary of the beginning of the Revolution there was a demonstration mass-strike of 200,000 workers. As in the days before the revolution in 1905, the flame broke out in June, in the Caucasus. In Baku, 40,000 workers were on a general strike. The flames leaped over to Petersburg. On the 17th of June 80,000 workers in Petersburg laid down their tools, on the 20th of July, 200,000 were out, July 23rd, the general strike movement was spreading out all over Russia, barricades were being built, the revolution was on its way. A few more months and it would have come, its flags fluttering in the wind. A few more years, and perhaps the whole world-political constellation would have been changed, imperialism, perhaps, would have received a firm check in its mad impulse.

But German reaction checked the revolutionary movement. From Berlin and Vienna came declarations of war, and the Russian revolution was buried beneath its wreckage. "German guns" are shattering, not Czarism, but its most dangerous enemy. The hopefully fluttering flag of the revolution sank down amid a wild whirlpool of war. But it sank honorably, and it will rise again out of the horrible massacre, in spite of "German guns," in spite of victory or defeat for Russia on the battlefields.

The national revolts in Russia which the Germans tried to foster, too, were unsuccessful. The Russian provinces were evidently less inclined to fall for the bait of Hindenburg's cohorts than the German Social-Democracy. The Jews, practical people that they are, were able to count out on their fingers that "German fists" which have been unable to overthrow their own Prussian reaction can hardly be expected to smash Russian absolutism. The Poles, exposed to the tripleheaded war, were not in the position to answer their "liberators" in audible language. But they will have remembered that Polish children were taught to pray the Lord's prayer in the German language with bloody welts on their backs, will not have forgotten the liberality of Prussian anti-Polish laws. All of them, Poles, Jews and Russians had no difficulty in understanding that the "German gun," when it descends upon their heads, brings not liberty, but death.

To couple the legend of Russian liberation with its Marxian heritage is worse than a poor joke on the part of the German Social-Democracy. It is a crime. To Marx, the Russian revolution was a turning point in the history of the world. Every political and historical perspective was made dependent upon the one consideration, "provided the Russian revolution has not already broken out." Marx believed in the Russian revolution and expected it even at a time when Russia was only a state of vassals. When the war broke out the Russian revolution had occurred. Its first attempt had not been victorious; but it could not be ignored; it is on the order of the day. And yet our German Social-Democrats came with "German guns," declaring the Russian revolution null and void; struck it from the pages of History. In 1848 Marx spoke from the German barricades; in Russia there was hopeless reaction. In 1914 Russia was in the throes of a revolution; while its German "liberators" were cowed by the fists of Prussian junkerdom.

But the liberating mission of the German armies was only an episode. German imperialism soon raised its uncomfortable mask and turned openly against France and England. Here, too, it was supported valiantly by a large number of the party papers. They ceased railing against the bloody Czar, and held up "perfidious Albion" and its merchant soul to the public disdain. They set out to free Europe, no longer from Russian absolutism, but from English naval supremacy. The hopeless confusion in which the party had become entangled, found a drastic illustration in the desperate attempt made by the more thoughtful portion of our party-press to meet this new change of front. In vain they tried to force the war back into its original channels, to nail it down to the "heritage of our masters"—that is, to the myth that they, the Social-Democracy—had themselves created "With heavy heart I have been forced to mobilize the army against a neighbor at whose side I have fought on so many battlefields. With honest sorrow I saw a friendship, truly served by Germany, break." That was simple, open, honest. But when the rhetoric of the first weeks of war backed down before the lapidary language of imperialism, the German Social-Democracy lost its only plausible excuse.

CHAPTER VI.

Of equal importance in the attitude of the Social-Democracy
was the official adoption of a program of civil peace, i. e. the
cessation of the class struggle for the duration of the war. The
declaration that was read by the Social-Democratic group in the
Reichstag on the fourth of August had been agreed upon in advance with representatives of the government and the capitalist
parties. It was little more than a patriotic grand-stand play,
prepared behind the scenes and delivered for the benefit of the
people at home and in other nations.

To the leading elements in the labor movement, the vote in
favor of the war credits by the Reichstag group was a cue for
the immediate settlement of all labor controversies. Nay more,
they announced this to the manufacturers as a patriotic duty incurred by labor when it agreed to observe a civil peace. These
same labor leaders undertook to supply city labor to farmers in
order to assure a prompt harvest. The leaders of the Social-
Democratic women's movement united with capitalist women for
"National service" and placed the most important elements that
remained after the mobilization at the disposal of national Samar-
itan work. Socialist women worked in soup kitchens and on ad-
visory commissions instead of carrying on agitation work for the
party. Under the socialist exception laws the party had utilized
parliamentary elections to spread its agitation and to keep a firm
hold upon the population in spite of the state of siege that had
been declared against the party and the persecution of the socialist press. In this crisis the social-democratic movement has
voluntarily relinquished all propaganda and education in the interest of the proletarian class struggle, during Reichstag and
Landtag elections. Parliamentary elections have everywhere
been reduced to the simple bourgeois formula; the catching of

votes for the candidates of the party on the basis of an amicable
and peaceful settlement with its capitalist opponents. When the
social-democratic representatives in the Landtag and in the muni-
cipal commissions—with the laudable exceptions of the Prussian
and the Alsatian Landtag—with high sounding references to the
existing state of civil peace, voted their approval of the war
credits that had been demanded, it only emphasized how completely the party had broken with things as they were before the war.
The social-democratic press, with a few exceptions, proclaimed
the principle of national unity as the highest duty of the German people. It warned the people not to withdraw their funds
from the savings banks lest by so doing they unbalance the economic life of the nation, and hinder the savings banks in liberally
buying war-loan bonds. It pleaded with proletarian women that
they should spare their husbands at the front the tales of suffering which they and their children were being forced to undergo,
to bear in silence the neglect of the government, to cheer the fighting warriors with happy stories of family life and favorable reports of prompt assistance through government agencies. They
rejoiced that the educational work that had been conducted for
so many years in and through the labor movement had become a
conspicuous asset in conducting the war. Something of this spirit
the following example will show:

"A friend in need is a friend indeed. This old adage has once
more proven its soundness. The social-democratic proletariat
that has been prosecuted and clubbed for its opinions went, like
one man, to protect our homes. German labor unions that had so
often suffered both in Germany and in Prussia report unanimously that the best of their members have joined the colors. Even
capitalist papers like the General-Anzeiger note the fact and express the conviction that "these people" will do their duty as well
as any man, that blows will rain most heavily where they stand."

"As for us, we are convinced that our labor unionists can do more than deal out blows. Modern mass armies have by no means simplified the work of their generals. It is practically impossible to move forward large troop divisions in close marching order under the deadly fire of modern artillery. Ranks must be carefully widened, must be more accurately controlled. Modern warfare requires discipline and clearness of vision not only in the divisions but in every individual soldier. The war will show how vastly human material has been improved by the educational work of the labor unions, how well their activity will serve the nation in these times of awful stress. The Russian and the French soldier may be capable of marvelous deeds of bravery. But in cool collected consideration none will surpass the German labor unionists. Then too, many of our organized workers know the ways and by-ways of the border land as well as they know their own pockets, and not a few of them are accomplished linguists. The Prussian advance in 1866 has been termed a schoolmasters' victory. This will be a victory of labor union leaders." (*Frankfurter Volksstimme*, August 18, 1914).

In the same strain the *Neue Zeit*, the theoretical organ of the party, declared (No. 23, Sept. 25, 1914) :

"Until the question of victory or defeat has been decided, all doubts must disappear, even as to the causes of the war. Today there can be no difference of party, class and nationality within the army or the population."

And in No. 8, Nov. 27, 1914, the same *Neue Zeit* declared in a chapter on "The Limitations of the International":

"The world war divides the socialists of the world into different camps and especially into different national camps. The International cannot prevent this. In other words, the International ceases to be an effective instrument in times of war. It is, on the whole, a peace instrument. Its great historic problem is the struggle for peace and the class struggle in times of peace."

Briefly, therefore, beginning with the fourth of August until the day when peace shall be declared, the social-democracy has declared the class struggle extinct. The first thunder of Krupp cannons in Belgium welded Germany into a wonderland of class solidarity and social harmony.

How is this miracle to be understood? The class struggle is known to be not a social-democratic invention that can be arbitrarily set aside for a period of time whenever it may seem convenient to do so. The proletarian class struggle is older than the social-democracy, is an elementary product of class society. It flamed up all over Europe when capitalism first came into power. The modern proletariat was not led by the social-democracy into the class struggle. On the contrary, the international social-democratic movement was called into being by the class struggle to bring a conscious aim and unity into the various local and scattered fragments of the class struggle. What then changed in this respect when the war broke out? Have private property, capitalist exploitation and class rule ceased to exist? Or have the propertied classes in a spell of patriotic fervor declared: in view of the needs of the war we hereby turn over the means of production, the earth, the factories and the mills thereon, into the possession of the people? Have they relinquished the right to make profits out of these possessions? Have they set aside all political privileges, will they sacrifice them upon the altar of the fatherland, now that it is in danger? It is, to say the least, a rather naive hypothesis, and sounds almost like a story from a kindergarten primer. And yet the declaration of our official leaders that the class struggle has been suspended, permits no other interpretation. Of course nothing of the sort has occurred. Property rights, exploitation and class rule, even political oppression in all its Prussian thoroughness have remained intact. The cannon in Belgium and in Eastern Prussia have not had the slightest influence upon the fundamental social and political structure of Germany.

The cessation of the class struggle was, therefore, a deplorably one-sided affair. While capitalist oppression and exploitation, the worst enemies of the working class remain, socialist and labor union leaders have generously delivered the working class, without a struggle, into the hands of the enemy for the duration of the war. While the ruling classes are fully armed with the property and supremacy rights, the working class, at the advice of the Social-Democracy has laid down its arms.

Once before, in 1848 in France, the proletariat experienced this miracle of class harmony, this fraternity of all classes of a modern capitalist state of society. In his "Class Struggles in France," Karl Marx writes: In the eyes of the proletariat, who confused the moneyed aristocracy with the bourgeoisie, in the imagination of republican idealists, who denied the very existence of classes, or attributed them to a monarchical form of government, in the deceitful phrases of those bourgeois who had hitherto been excluded from power, the rule of the bourgeoisie was ended when the republic was proclaimed. At that time all royalists became republican, all millionaires in Paris became laborers. In the word "Fraternité," the brotherhood of man, this imaginary destruction of classes found official expression. This comfortable abstraction from class differences, this sentimental balancing of class interests, this utopian disregard of the class struggle, this "Fraternité" was the real slogan of the February revolution. . . The Parisian proletariat rejoiced in an orgy of brotherhood. . . The Parisian proletariat, looking upon the republic as its own creation, naturally acclaimed every act of the provisional bourgeois government. Willingly it permitted Caussidiere to use its members as policemen to protect the property of Paris. With unquestioning faith it allowed Louis Blanc to regulate wage differences betwen workers and masters. In their eyes it was a matter of honor to preserve the fair name of the republic before the peoples of Europe."

Thus in February, 1848, a naive Parisian proletariat set aside the class struggle. But let us not forget that even they committed this mistake only after the July monarchy had been crushed by their revolutionary action, after a republic had been established. The fourth of August, 1914, is an inverted February revolution: It is the setting aside of class differences, not under a republic, but under a military monarchy, not after a victory of the people over reaction, but after a victory of reaction over the people, not with the proclamation of "Liberté, Egalité, Fraternité," but with the proclamation of a state of siege, after the press had been choked and the constitution annihilated.

Impressively the government of Germany proclaimed a civil peace. Solemnly the parties promised to abide by it. But as experienced politicians these gentlemen know full well that it is fatal to trust too much to promises. They secured civil peace for themselves by the very real measure of a military dictatorship. This too the social-democratic group accepted without protest or opposition. In the declarations of August fourth and December second there is not a syllable of indignation over the affront contained in the proclamation of military rule. When it voted for civil peace and war credits, the social-democracy silently gave its consent to military rule as well, and laid itself, bound and gagged, at the feet of the ruling classes. The declaration of military rule was purely an anti-socialist measure. From no other side were resistance, protest, action, and difficulties to be expected. As a reward for its capitulation the social-democracy merely received what it would have received under any circumstances, even after an unsuccessful resistance, namely military rule. The impressive declaration of the Reichstag group emphasizes the old socialist principle of the right of nations to self-determination, as an explanation of their vote in favor of war credits. Self-determination for the German proletariat was the straight-jacket of a state of siege. Never in the history of the world has a party made itself more ridiculous.

But more! In refuting the existence of the class struggle, the social-democracy has denied the very basis of its own existence. What is the very breath of its body, if not the class struggle? What role could it expect to play in the war, once having sacrificed the class struggle, the fundamental principle of its existence? The social-democracy has destroyed its mission, for the period of the war, as an active political party, as a representative of working class politics. It has thrown aside the most important weapon it possessed, the power of criticism of the war from the peculiar point of view of the working class. Its only mission now is to play the role of the gendarme over the working class under a state of military rule.

German freedom, that same German freedom for which, according to the declaration of the Reichstag group, Krupp cannons are now fighting, has been endangered by this attitude of the social-democracy far beyond the period of the present war. The leaders of the Social-Democracy are convinced that democratic liberties for the working class will come as a reward for its allegiance to the fatherland. But never in the history of the world has an oppressed class received political rights as a reward for service rendered to the ruling classes. History is full of examples of shameful deceit on the part of the ruling classes, even when solemn promises were made before the war broke out. The Social-Democracy has not assured the extension of liberty in Germany. It has sacrificed those liberties that the working class possessed before the war broke out. The indifference with which the German people have allowed themselves to be deprived of the freedom of the press, of the right of assembly and of public life, the fact that they not only calmly bore, but even applauded the state of siege, is unexampled in the history of modern society. In England the freedom of the press has nowhere been violated, in France there is incomparably more freedom of public opinion than in Germany. In no country has public opinion so

completely vanished, nowhere has it been so completely superseded by official opinion, by the order of the government, as in
Germany. Even in Russia there is only the destructive work of
a public censor who effectively wipes out opposition of opinion.
But not even there have they descended to the custom of providing articles ready for the press to the opposition papers. In no
other country has the government forced the opposition press to
express in its columns the politics that have been dictated and
ordered by the government in "Confidential Conferences." Such
measures were unknown even in Germany during the war of
1870. At that time the press enjoyed unlimited freedom, and accompanied the events of the war, to Bismarck's active resentment, with criticism that was often exceedingly sharp. The
newspapers were full of active discussion on war aims, on questions of annexation, and constitutionality. When Johann Jacobi
was arrested, a storm of indignation swept over Germany, so
that even Bismarck felt obliged to disavow all responsibility for
this "mistake" of the powers of reaction. Such was the situation
in Germany at a time when Bebel and Liebknecht, in the name
of the German working class, had declined all community of
interests with the ruling jingoes. It took a Social-Democracy with
four and one-half million votes to conceive of the touching
"Burgfrieden," to assent to war credits, to bring upon us the
worst military dictatorship that was ever suffered to exist. That
such a thing is possible in Germany to-day, that not only the bourgeois press, but the highly developed and influential socialist press
as well permits these things without even the pretence of opposition bears a fatal significance for the future of Germany liberty.
It proves that society in Germany to-day has within itself no
foundation for political freedom, since it allows itself to be thus
lightly deprived of its most sacred rights. Let us not forget that
the political rights that existed in Germany before the war were
not won, as were those of France and England, in great and re-

peated revolutionary struggles, are not firmly anchored in the lives of the people by the power of revolutionary tradition. They are the gift of a Bismarckian policy granted after a period of victorious counter-revolution that lasted over twenty years. German liberties did not ripen on the field of revolution, they are the product of diplomatic gambling by Prussian military monarchy, they are the cement with which this military monarchy has united the present German empire. Danger threatens the free development of German freedom not, as the German Reichstag group believe, from Russia, but in Germany itself. It lies in the peculiar counter-revolutionary origin of the German constitution, and looms dark in the reactionary powers that have controlled the German state since the empire was founded, conducting a silent but relentless war against these pitiful "German liberties." The Junkers of east of the Elbe, the business jingoes, the arch-reactionaries of the Center, the degraded "German liberals," the personal rulership, the sway of the sword, the Zabern policy, that triumphed all over Germany before the war broke out, these are the real enemies of culture and liberty, and the war, the state of siege and the attitude of the social democracy, are strengthening the powers of darkness all over the land. The Liberal, to be sure, can explain away this graveyard quiet in Germany with a characteristically liberal explanation; to him it is only a temporary sacrifice, for the duration of the war. But to a people that is politically ripe, a sacrifice of its rights and its public life, even temporarily, is as impossible as for a human being to give up, for a time, his right to breathe. A people that gives silent consent to military government in times of war thereby admits that political independence at any time is superfluous. The passive submission of the Social Democracy to the present state of siege and its vote for war credits without attaching the slightest condition thereto, its acceptance of a civil peace, has demoralized the masses, the only existing pillar of German constitutional government, has strengthened the reaction of its rulers, the enemies of constitutional government.

By sacrificing the class struggle our party has moreover, once and for all, given up the possibility of making its influence effectively felt in determining the extent of the war and the terms of peace.   To its own official declaration, its acts have been a stinging blow.   While protesting against all annexations, which are, after all, the logical consequences of an imperialistic war that is successful from the military point of view, it has handed over every weapon that the working class possessed that might have empowered the masses to mobilize public opinion in their own direction, to exert an effective pressure upon the terms of war and of peace.   By assuring militarism of peace and quiet at home the Social Democracy has given its military rulers permission to follow their own course without even considering the interests of the masses, has unleashed in the hearts of the ruling classes the most unbridled imperialistic tendencies.   In other words, when the Social Democracy adopted its platform of civil peace, and the political disarmament of the working class, it condemned its own demand of no annexations to impotency.

Thus the Social Democracy has added another crime to the heavy burden it already has to bear, namely the lengthening of the war.   The commonly accepted dogma that we can oppose the war only so long as it is threatened, has become a dangerous trap. As an inevitable consequence, once the war has come, social democratic political action is at an end.   There can be, then, but one question, victory or defeat, i. e., the class struggle must stop for the period of the war.   But actually the greatest problem for the political movement of the Social Democracy begins only after the war has broken out.   At the international congresses held in Stuttgart in 1907 and in Basel in 1912, the German party and labor union leaders unanimously voted in favor of a resolution which says:

"Should war nevertheless break out, it shall be the duty of the Social-Democracy to work for a speedy peace, and to strive with every means in its power to utilize the industrial and political crisis to accomplish the awakening of the people, thus hastening the overthrow of capitalist class rule".

What has the Social-Democracy done in this war? Exactly the contrary. By voting in favor of war credits and entering upon a civil peace, it has striven, by all the means in its power, to prevent the industrial and political crisis, to prevent an awakening of the masses by the war. It strives "with all the means in its power" to save the capitalist state from its own anarchy, to reduce the number of its victims. It is claimed—we have often heard this argument used by Reichstag deputies—that not one man less would have fallen upon the battle fields if the Social Democratic group had voted against the war credits. Our party press has steadfastly maintained that we must support and join in the defence of our country in order to reduce the number of bloody victims that this war shall cost. But the policy that we have followed out has had exactly the opposite effect. In the first place, thanks to the civil peace, and the patriotic attitude of the Social Democracy, the imperialistic war unleashed its furies without fear. Hitherto, fear of restiveness at home, fear of the fury of the hungry populace, have been a load upon the minds of the ruling classes that effectively checked them in their bellicose desires. In the well known words of Buelow: "they are trying to put off the war chiefly because they fear the Social Democracy". Rohrbach says in his "Krieg und die Deutsche Politik", page 7, "unless elemental catastrophies intervene, the only power that can force Germany to make peace is the hunger of the breadless". Obviously he meant a hunger that attracts attention, that forces itself unpleasantly upon the ruling classes in order to force them to pay heed to its demands. Let us see, finally, what a prominent military theoretician, General Bernhardi, says, in his great work "Vom Heutigen Kriege." "Thus modern mass armies make war difficult for a variety of reasons. Moreover they constitute, in and of themselves, a danger that must never be underestimated.

"The mechanism of such an army is so huge and so complicated that it can remain efficient and flexible only so long as its cogs and wheels work, in the main, dependably, and obvious moral confusion is carefully prevented. These are things that cannot be completely avoided, as little as we can conduct a war exclusively with victorious battles. They can be overcome if they appear only within certain restricted limits. But when great, compact masses once shake off their leaders, when a spirit of panic becomes widespread, when a lack of sustenance becomes extensively felt, when the spirit of revolt spreads out among the masses of the army, then the army becomes not only ineffectual against the enemy, it becomes a menace to itself and to its leaders. When the army bursts the bands of discipline, when it voluntarily interrupts the course of military operation, it creates problems that its leaders are unable to solve.

"War, with its modern mass armies is, under all circumstances, a dangerous game, a game that demands the greatest possible personal and financial sacrifice the state can offer. Under such circumstances it is clear that provision must be made everywhere that the war, once it has broken out, be brought to an end as quickly as possible, to release the extreme tension that must accompany this supreme effort on the part of whole nations."

Thus capitalist politicians and military authorities alike believe war, with its modern mass armies, to be a dangerous game. And therein lay for the Social Democracy the most effectual op-

portunity, to prevent the rulers of the present day from precipit-
ating war and to force them to end it as rapidly as possible. But
the position of the Social Democracy in this war cleared away
all doubts, has torn down the dams that held back the storm-
flood of militarism. In fact it has created a power for which
neither Bernhardi nor any other capitalist statesman dared hope
in his wildest dreams. From the camp of the social-democrats
came the cry: "Durchhalten", i. e., a continuation of this human
slaughter. And so the thousands of victims that have fallen
for months on the battlefields lie upon our conscience.

CHAPTER VII.

"But since we have been unable to prevent the war, since it has come in spite of us, and our country is facing invasion, shall we leave our country defenseless! Shall we deliver it into the hands of the enemy? Does not Socialism demand the right of nations to determine their own destinies? Does it not mean that every people is justified, nay more, is in duty bound, to protect its liberties, its independence? 'When the house is on fire, shall we not first try to put out the blaze before stopping to ascertain the incendiary?' "

These arguments have been repeated, again and again in defense of the attitude of the Social-Democracy, in Germany and in France.

Even in the neutral countries this argument has been used. Translated into Dutch we read for instance: "When the ship leaks must we not seek, first of all, to stop the hole?"

To be sure. Fie upon a people that capitulates before invasion and fie upon a party that capitulates before the enemy within.

But there is one thing that the fireman in the burning house has forgotten: that in the mouth of a Socialist the phrase "Defending one's fatherland" cannot mean playing the role of cannon fodder under the command of an imperialistic bourgeoisie.

Is an invasion really the horror of all horrors, before which all class conflict within the country must subside as though spellbound by some supernatural witchcraft? According to the police theory of bourgeois patriotism and military rule, every evidence of the class struggle is a crime against the interests of the country because they maintain that it constitutes a weakening of the stamina of the nation. The Social-Democracy has allowed itself to be perverted into this same distorted point of view. Has not the history of modern capitalist society shown that in the eyes of capitalist society, foreign invasion is by no means the unmitigated terror as which it is generally painted; that on the contrary it is a measure to which the bourgeoisie has frequently and gladly resorted as an effective weapon against the enemy within? Did not the Bourbons and the aristocrats of France invite foreign invasion against the Jacobites? Did not the Austrian counter-revolution in 1849 call out the French invaders against Rome, the Russian against Budapest? Did not the "Party of Law and Order" in France in 1850 openly threaten an invasion of the Cossacks in order to bring the national assembly to terms? And was not the Bonaparte army released, and the support of the Prussian army against the Paris Commune assured, by the famous contract between Jules Favre, Thiers and Co., and Bismarck? This historical evidence led Karl Marx, 45 years ago, to expose the "national wars" of modern capitalist society as miserable frauds. In his famous address to the General Council of the International on the downfall of the Paris Commune, he said:

"That, after the greatest war of modern times the belligerent armies, the victor and the vanquished, should unite for the mutual butchery of the proletariat—this incredible event proves, not as Bismarck would have us believe, the final overthrow of the new social power—but the complete disintegration of the old bourgeois society. The highest heroic accomplishment of which the old order is capable, is the national war. And this has now proved to be a fraud perpetrated by government for no other purpose than to put off the class struggle, a fraud that is bared as soon as the class struggle flares up in a civil war. Class rule can no longer hide behind a national uniform. The national governments are united against the proletariat."

In capitalist history, invasion and class struggle are not opposites, as the official legend would have us believe, but one is the means and the expression of the other. Just as invasion is the true and tried weapon in the hands of capital against the class struggle, so on the other hand the fearless pursuit of the class struggle has always proven the most effective preventative of foreign invasions. On the brink of modern times are the examples of the Italian cities, Florence, and Milano, with their century of bitter struggle against the Hohenstaufen. The stormy history of these cities, torn by inner conflicts, proves that the force and the fury of inner class struggles not only does not weaken the defensive powers of the community, but that on the contrary, from their fires shoot the only flames that are strong enough to withstand every attack from a foreign foe.

But the classic example of our own times is the great French Revolution. In 1793 Paris, the heart of France, was surrounded by enemies. And yet Paris and France at that time did not succumb to the invasion of a stormy flood of European coalition; on the contrary, it welded its force in the face of the growing danger, to a more gigantic opposition. If France, at that critical time, was able to meet each new coalition of the enemy with a new miraculous loosening of the inmost forces of society in the great miraculous and undiminished fighting spirit, it was only because of the impetuous loosening of the inmost forces of society in the great struggle of the classes of France. Today, in the perspective of a century, it is clearly discernible that only this intensification of the class struggle, that only the Dictatorship of the French people and their fearless radicalism, could produce means and forces out of the soil of France, sufficient to defend and to sustain a new-born society against a world of enemies, against the intrigues of a dynasty, against the traitorous machinations of the aristocrats, against the attempts of the clergy, against the treachery of their generals, against the opposition of sixty departments and provincial capitals, and against the united armies and navies of monarchial Europe. The centuries have proven that not the state of siege, but relentless class struggle is the power that awakens the spirit of self-sacrifice, the moral strength of the masses, that the class struggle is the best protection and the best defense against a foreign enemy.

This same tragic quidproquo victimized the Social-Democracy when it based its attitude in this war upon the doctrine of the right of national self-determination.

It is true that Socialism gives to every people the right of independence and the freedom of independent control of its own destinies. But it is a veritable perversion of Socialism to regard present day capitalist society as the expression of this self-determination of nations. Where is there a nation in which the people have had the right to determine the form and conditions of their national, political and social existence? In Germany the determination of the people found concrete expression in the demands formulated by the German revolutionary democrats of 1848; the first fighters of the German proletariat, Marx, Engels, Lassalle, Bebel and Liebknecht, proclaimed and fought for a united German Republic. For this ideal the revolutionary forces in Berlin and in Vienna, in those tragic days of March, shed their heart's blood upon the barricades. To carry out this program, Marx and Engels demanded that Prussia take up arms against Czarism. The foremost demand made in the national program was for the liquidation of "the heap of organized decay, the Hapsburg monarchy," as well as of two dozen other dwarf monarchies within Germany itself. The overthrow of the German revolution, the treachery of the German bourgeoisie to its own democratic ideals, led to the Bismarck regime and to its creature, present-day Greater Prussia, twenty-five fatherlands under one helm, the German empire. Modern Germany is built upon the grave of the March Revolution, upon the wreckage of the right of self-determination of the German people. The present war, supporting Turkey and the Hapsburg monarchy, and strengthening German military autocracy is a second burial of the March revolutionists, and of the national program of the German people.

It is a fiendish jest of history that the Social-Democrats, the heirs of the German patriots of 1848, should go forth in this war with the banner of "self-determination of nations" held aloft in their hands. But, perhaps the third French Republic, with its colonial possessions in four continents and its colonial horrors in two, is the expression of the self-determination of the French nation? Or the British nation, with its India, with its South African rule of a million whites over a population of five million colored people? Or perhaps Turkey, or the Empire of the Czar?

Capitalist politicians, in whose eyes the rulers of the people and the ruling classes are the nation, can honestly speak of the "right of national self-determination" in connection with such colonial empires. To the Socialist, no nation is free whose national existence is based upon the enslavement of another people, for to him colonial peoples, too, are human beings, and, as such, parts of the national state. International Socialism recognizes the right of free independent nations, with equal rights. But Socialism alone can create such nations, can bring self-determination of their peoples. This slogan of Socialism is like all its others, not an apology for existing conditions, but a guide-post, a spur for the revolutionary, regenerative, active policy of the proletariat. So long as capitalist states exist, i. e., so long as imperialistic world policies determine and regulate the inner and the outer life of a nation, there can be no "national self-determination" either in war or in peace.

In the present imperialistic milieu there can be no wars of national self-defense. Every socialist policy that depends upon this determining historic milieu, that is willing to fix its policies in the world whirlpool from the point of view of a single nation is built upon a foundation of sand.

We have already attempted to show the background for the present conflict between Germany and her opponents. It was necessary to show up more clearly the actual forces and relations

that constitute the motive power behind the present war, because
this legend of the defense of the existence, the freedom and
civilization of Germany plays an important part in the attitude of
our group in the Reichstag and our Socialist press.
Against this legend historical truth must be emphasized to show
that this is a war that has been prepared by German militarism
and its world-political ideas for years, that it was brought about
in the Summer of 1914, by Austrian and German diplomacy, with
a full realization of its import.

In a discussion of the general causes of the war, and of its
significance, the question of the "guilty party" is completely
beside the issue. Germany certainly has not the right to speak of
a war of defense, but France and England have little more
justification. They too, are protecting, not their national, but their
world-political existence, their old imperialistic possessions, from
the attacks of the German upstart. Doubtless the raids of German and Austrian imperialism in the Orient started the conflagration, but French imperialism, by devouring Morocco, and
English imperialism, in its attempts to rape Mesopotamia, and all
the other measures that were calculated to secure its rule of force
in India, Russia's Baltic policies, aiming toward Constantinople,
all of these factors have carried together and piled up, brand for
brand, the firewood that feeds the conflagration. If capitalist
armaments have played an important role as the mainspring that
times the outbreak of the catastrophe, it was a competition of
armaments in all nations. And if Germany laid the cornerstone
for European competitive armaments by Bismarck's policy of
1870, this policy was furthered by that of the second Empire and
by the military-colonial policies of the third empire, by its ex-
pansions in East Asia and in Africa.

The French Socialists have some slight foundation for their
illusion of "national defense," because neither the French government nor the French people entertained the slightest warlike
desires in July 1914. "Today everyone in France is honestly,

uprightly and without reservation for peace," insisted Jaurès in the last speech of his life, on the eve of the war, when he addressed a meeting in the People's House in Brussels. This was absolutely true, and gives the psychological explanation for the indignation of the French Socialists when this criminal war was forced upon their country. But this fact was not sufficient to determine the Socialist attitude on the world war as an historic occurrence.

The events that bore the present war did not begin in July 1914 but reach back for decades. Thread by thread they have been woven together on the loom of an inexorable natural development, until the firm net of imperialist world politics has encircled five continents. It is a huge historical complex of events, whose roots reach deep down into the Plutonic deeps of economic creation, whose outermost branches spread out and point away into a dimly dawning new world, events before whose all-embracing immensity, the conception of guilt and retribution, of defense and offense, sink into pale nothingness.

Imperialism is not the creation of any one or of any group of states. It is the product of a particular stage of ripeness in the world development of capital, an innately international condition, an indivisible whole, that is recognizable only in all its relations, and from which no nation can hold aloof at will. From this point of view only is it possible to understand correctly the question of "national defense" in the present war.

The national state, national unity and independence were the ideological shield under which the capitalist nations of central Europe constituted themselves in the past century. Capitalism is incompatible with economic and political divisions, with the accompanying splitting up into small states. It needs for its development large, united territories, and a state of mental and intellectual development in the nation that will lift the demands and needs of society to a plane corresponding to the prevailing stage of capitalistic production, and to the mechanism of modern capitalist class rule. Before capitalism could develop, it sought to create for itself a territory sharply defined by national limitations. This program was carried out only in France at the time of the great revolution, for in the national and political heritage left to Europe by the feudal middle ages, this could be accomplished only by revolutionary measures. In the rest of Europe this nationalization, like the revolutionary movement as a whole, remained the patchwork of half-kept promises. The German empire, modern Italy, Austria-Hungary, and Turkey, the Russian Empire and the British world-empire, are all living proofs of this fact. The national program could play a historic role only so long as it represented the ideological expression of a growing bourgeoisie, lusting for power, until it had fastened its class rule, in some way or other, upon the great nations of central Europe and had created within them the necessary tools and conditions of its growth. Since then, imperialism has buried the old bourgeois democratic program completely by substituting expansionistic activity irrespective of national relationships for the original program of the bourgeoisie in all nations. The national phrase, to be sure, has been preserved, but its real content, its function has been perverted into its very opposite. Today the nation is but a cloak that covers imperialistic desires, a battle cry for imperialistic rivalries, the last ideological measure with which the masses can be persuaded to play the role of cannon fodder in imperialistic wars.

This general tendency of present day capitalist policies determines the policies of the individual states as their supreme blindly operating law, just as the laws of economic competition determine the conditions under which the individual manufacturer shall produce.

Let us assume for a moment, for the sake of argument, for the purpose of investigating this phantom of "national wars" that controls Social-Democratic politics at the present time, that in one of the belligerent states, the war at its outbreak was purely one of national defense. Military success would immediately demand the occupation of foreign territory. But the existence of influential capitalist groups, interested in imperialistic annexations, will awaken expansionistic appetites as the war goes on. The imperialistic tendency that, at the beginning of hostilities, may have been existent only in embryo, will shoot up and expand in the hothouse atmosphere of war until they will in a short time, determine its character, its aims and its results. Furthermore, the system of alliance between military states that has ruled the political relations of these nations for decades in the past, makes it inevitable that each of the belligerent parties in the course of war, should try to bring its allies to its assistance, again purely from motives of self-defense. Thus one country after another is drawn into the war, inevitably new imperialistic circles are touched and others are created. Thus England drew in Japan, and, spreading the war into Asia, has brought China into the circle of political problems and has influenced the existing rivalry between Japan and the United States, between England and Japan, thus heaping up new material for future conflicts. Thus Germany has dragged Turkey into the war, bringing the question of Constantinople, of the Balkans and of Western Asia directly into the foreground of affairs. Even he who did not realize at the outset that the world war, in its causes, was purely imperialistic, cannot fail to see after a dispassionate view of its effects that war, under the present conditions, automatically and inevitably develops into a process of world division. This was apparent from the very first. The wavering balance of power between the two belligerent parties forces each, if only for military reasons, in order to strengthen its own position, or in order to frustrate possible attacks, to hold the neutral nations in check by intensive deals in peoples and nations, such as the German-Austrian offers to Italy, Rumania, Bulgaria and Greece on the one hand, and the English-Russian bids on the other. The "National war of defense" has the surprising effect of creating, even in the neutral nations, a general transformation of ownership and relative power, always in direct line with expansionistic tendencies. Finally the fact that all modern capitalist states have colonial possessions that will, even though the war may have begun as a war of national defense, be drawn into the conflict from purely military considerations, the fact that each country will strive to occupy the colonial possessions of its opponent, or at least to create disturbances therein, automatically turns every war into an imperialistic world conflagration.

Thus the conception of even that modest, devout fatherland-loving war of defense that has become the ideal of our parliamentarians and editors is pure fiction, and shows, on their part, a complete lack of understanding of the whole war and its world relations. The character of the war is determined, not by solemn declaration, not even by the honest intentions of leading politicians, but by the momentary configuration of society and its military organizations. At the first glance the term "national war of defense" might seem applicable in the case of a country like Switzerland. But Switzerland is no national state, and, therefore, no object of comparison with other modern states. Its very "neutral" existence, its luxury of a militia, are after all only the negative fruits of a latent state of war in the surrounding great military states. It will hold this neutrality only so long as it is willing to oppose this condition. How quickly such a neutral state is crushed by the military heel of imperialism in a world war the fate of Belgium shows. This brings us to the peculiar position of the "small nation." A classic example of such "national wars" is Servia. If ever a state, according to formal considerations, had the right of national defense on its side, that state is Servia. Deprived through Austrian annexations of its national unity, threatened by Austria in its very existence as a nation, forced by Austria into war, it is fighting, according to all human conceptions, for existence, for freedom and for the civilization of its people. But if the Social-Democratic group is right in its position, then the Servian Social-Democrats who protested against the war in the parliament at Belgrade and refused to vote war credits are actually traitors to the most vital interests of their own nation. In reality the Servian Socialists Lapschewitsh and Kanzlerowitsh have not only enrolled their names in letters of gold in the annals of the international socialist movement, but have shown a clear historical conception of the real causes of the war. In voting against war credits they therefore have done their country the best possible service. Servia is formally engaged in a national war of defense. But its monarchy and its ruling classes are filled with expansionist desires as are the ruling classes in all modern states. They are indifferent to ethnic lines, and thus their warfare assumes an aggressive character. Thus Servia is today reaching out toward the Adriatic coast where it is fighting out a real imperialistic conflict with Italy on the backs of the Albanians, a conflict whose final outcome will be decided not by either of the powers directly interested, but by the great powers that will speak the last word on terms of peace. But above all this we must not forget: behind Servian nationalism stands Russian imperialism. Servia itself is only a pawn in the great game of world politics. A judgment of the war in Servia from a point of view that fails to take these great relations and the general world-political background into account, is necessarily without foundation. The same is true of the recent Balkan War. Regarded as an isolated occurrence, the young Balkan States were historically justified in defending the old democratic program of the national state. In their historical connection, however, which makes the Balkan the burning point and the center of imperialistic world policies, these Balkan wars, also, were objectively only a fragment of the general conflict, a link in the chain of events that led, with fatal necessity, to the present world war. After the Balkan war the international Social-Democracy tendered to the Balkan Socialists, for their determined refusal to offer moral or political support to the war, a most enthusiastic ovation at the peace congress at Basel. In this act alone the International condemned in advance the position taken by the German and French Socialists in the present war.

All small states, as for instance Holland, are today in a position like that of the Balkan states. "When the ship leaks, the hole must be stopped"; and what, forsooth, could little Holland fight for but for its national existence and for the independence of its people? If we consider here merely the determination of the Dutch people, even of its ruling classes, the question is doubtlessly one purely of national defense. But again proletarian politics cannot judge according to the subjective purposes of a single country. Here again it must take its position as a part of the International, according to the whole complexity of the world's political situation. Holland, too, whether it wishes to be or not, is only a small wheel in the great machine of modern world politics and diplomacy. This would become clear at once, if Holland were actually torn into the maelstrom of the world war. Its opponents would direct their attacks against its colonies. Automatically Dutch warfare would turn to the defense of its present possessions. The defense of the national independence of the Dutch people on the North Sea would expand concretely to the defense of its rule and right of exploitation over the Malays in the East Indian Archipelago. But not enough: Dutch militarism, if forced to rely upon itself, would be crushed like a nutshell in the whirlpool of the world war. Whether it wished to or not it would become a member of one of the great national alliances. On one side or the other it must be the bearer and the tool of purely imperialistic tendencies.

Thus it is always the historic milieu of modern imperialism that determines the character of the war in the individual countries, and this milieu makes a war of national self-defense impossible.

Kautsky also expressed this, only a few years ago, in his pamphlet "Patriotism and Social-Democracy," Leipzig, 1907:

"Though the patriotism of the bourgeoisie and of the proletariat are two entirely different, actually opposite phenomena, there are situations in which both kinds of patriotism may join forces for united action, even in times of war. The bourgeoisie and the proletariat of a nation are equally interested in their national independence and self-determination, in the removal of all kinds of oppression and exploitation at the hands of a foreign nation. In the national conflicts that have sprung from such attempts, the patriotism of the proletariat has always united with that of the bourgeoisie. But the proletariat has become a power that may become dangerous to the ruling classes at every great national upheaval; revolution looms dark at the end of every war, as the Paris Commune of 1871 and Russian terrorism after the Russian-Japanese war have proven. In view of this the bourgeoisie of those nations which are not sufficiently united have actually sacrificed their national aims where these can be maintained only at the expense of their government, for they hate and fear the revolution even more than they love national independence and greatness. For this reason, the bourgeoisie sacrifices the independence of Poland and permits ancient constellations like Austria and Turkey to remain in existence, though they have been doomed to destruction for more than a generation. National struggles as the bringers of revolution have ceased in civilized Europe. National problems that today can be solved only by war or revolution, will be solved in the future only by the victory of the proletariat. But then, thanks to international solidarity, they will at once assume a form entirely different from that which prevails today in a social state of exploitation and oppression. In capitalistic states this problem needs no longer to trouble the proletariat in its practical struggles. It must divert its whole strength to other problems." (Page 12-14.)

"Meanwhile the likelihood that proletarian and bourgeois patriotism will unite to protect the liberty of the people is becoming more and more rare." Kautsky then goes on to say that the French bourgeoisie has united with Czarism, that Russia has ceased to be a danger for western Europe because it has been weakened by the Revolution. "Under these circumstances a war in defense of national liberty in which bourgeois and proletarian may unite, is nowhere to be expected." (Page 16.)

"We have already seen that conflicts which, in the 19th century, might still have led some liberty loving peoples to oppose their neighbors, by warfare, have ceased to exist. We have seen that modern militarism nowhere aims to defend important popular rights, but everywhere strives to support profits. Its activities are dedicated not to assure the independence and invulnerability of its own nationality, that is nowhere threatened, but to the assurance and the extension of over-sea conquests that again only serve the aggrandizement of capitalist profits. At the present time the conflicts between states can bring no war that proletarian interests would not, as a matter of duty, energetically oppose." (Page 23.)

In view of all these considerations, what shall be the practical attitude of the Social-Democracy in the present war? Shall it declare: since this is an imperialistic war, since we do not enjoy in our country, any Socialist self-determination, its existence or non-existence is of no consequence to us, and we will surrender it to the enemy? Passive fatalism can never be the role of a revolutionary party, like the Social-Democracy. It must neither place itself at the disposal of the existing class state, under the command of the ruling classes, nor can it stand silently by to wait until the storm is past. It must adopt a policy of active class politics, a policy that will whip the ruling classes forward in every great social crisis, and that will drive the crisis itself far beyond its original extent. That is the role that the Social-Democracy must play as the leader of the fighting proletariat. Instead of covering this imperialistic war with a lying mantle of national self-defense, the Social-Democracy should have demanded the right of national self-determination seriously, should have used it as a lever against the imperialistic war.

The most elementary demand of national defense is that the nation take its defense into its own hands. The first step in this direction is the militia; not only the immediate armament of the entire adult male populace, but above all, popular decision in all questions of peace and war. It must demand, furthermore, the immediate removal of every form of political oppression, since the greatest political freedom is the best basis for national defense. To proclaim these fundamental measures of national defense, to demand their realization, that was the first duty of the Social-Democracy.

For forty years we have tried to prove to the ruling classes as well as to the masses of the people that only the militia is really able to defend the fatherland and to make it invincible. And yet, when the first test came, we turned over the defense of our country, as a matter of course, into the hands of a standing army, to be the cannon fodder under the club of the ruling classes. Our parliamentarians apparently did not even notice that the fervent wishes with which they sped these defenders of the fatherland to the front were, to all intents and purposes, an open admission that the imperial Prussian standing army is the real defender of the fatherland. They evidently did not realize that by this admission they sacrificed the fulcrum of our political program, that they gave up the militia and dissolved the practical significance of forty years' of agitation against the standing army into thin air. By the act of the Social-Democratic group our military program became a utopian doctrine, a doctrinaire obsession, that none could possibly take seriously.

The masters of the international proletariat saw the idea of fatherland defense in a different light. When the proletariat of Paris, surrounded by Prussians in 1871, took the reins of the government into its own hands, Marx wrote enthusiastically:

"Paris, the center and seat of the old government powers, and simultaneously the social center of gravity of the French working class, Paris has risen in arms against the attempt of Monsieur Thiers and his Junkers to reinstate and perpetuate the government of the old powers of imperial rule. Paris was in a position to resist only, because, through the state of siege, it was rid of its army, because in its place there had been put a national guard composed chiefly of working men. It was necessary that this innovation be made a permanent institution. The first act of the Commune was, therefore, the suppression of the standing army and the substitution of an armed people. . . . If now, the Commune was the true representative of all healthy elements of French society and, therefore, a true national government, it was likewise, as a proletarian government, as the daring fighter for the liberation of labor, international in the truest sense of that word. Under the eyes of the Prussian army, which has annexed two French Provinces to Germany, the Commune has annexed the workers of a whole world to France." (Address of the General Council of the International.)

But what did our masters say concerning the role to be played by the Social-Democracy in the present war? In 1892 Friedrich Engels expressed the following opinion concerning the fundamental lines along which the attitude of proletarian parties in a great war should follow:

"A war in the course of which Russians and Frenchmen should invade Germany would mean for the latter a life and death struggle. Under such circumstances it could assure its national existence only by using the most revolutionary methods. The present government, should it not be forced to do so, will certainly not bring on the revolution, but we have a strong party that may force its hand, or that, should it be necessary, can replace it, the Social-Democratic party.

"We have not forgotten the glorious example of France in 1793.

The one hundredth anniversary of 1793 is approaching. Should Russia's desire for conquest, or the chauvinistic impatience of the French Bourgeoisie, check the victorious but peaceable march of the German Socialists, the latter are prepared—be assured of that—to prove to the world that the German proletarians of today are not unworthy of the French Sansculottes, that 1893 will be worthy of 1793. And should the soldiers of Monsieur Constans set foot upon German territory we will meet them with the words of the Marseillaise:

> "Shall hateful tyrants, mischief breeding,
> With hireling host, a ruffian band,
> Affright and desolate the land?"

"In short, peace assures the victory of the Social-Democratic party in about ten years. The war will bring either victory in two or three years or its absolute ruin for at least fifteen or twenty years."

When Engels wrote these words, he had in mind a situation entirely different from the one existing today. In his mind's eye, ancient Czarism still loomed threateningly in the background. We have already seen the great Russian Revolution. He thought, furthermore, of a real national war of defense, of a Germany attacked on two sides, on the East and on the West by two enemy forces. Finally, he overestimated the ripeness of conditions in Germany and the likelihood of a social revolution, as all true fighters are wont to overrate the real tempo of development. But for all that, his sentences prove with remarkable clearness, that Engels meant by national, defense in the sense of the Social-Democracy, not the support of a Prussian Junker military government and its Generalstab, but a revolutionary action after the example of the French Jacobites.

Yes, Socialists should defend their country in great historical crises, and here lies the great fault of the German Social-Democratic Reichstag group. When it announced on the 4th of August, "in this hour of danger, we will not desert our fatherland," it denied its own words in the same breath. For truly it has deserted its fatherland in its hour of greatest danger, The highest duty of the Social-Democracy toward its fatherland demanded that it expose the real background of this imperialistic war, that it rend the net of imperialistic and diplomatic lies that covers the eyes of the people. It was their duty to speak loudly and clearly, to proclaim to the people of Germany that in this war victory and defeat would be equally fatal, to oppose the gagging of the fatherland by a state of siege, to demand that the people alone decide on war and peace, to demand a permanent session of Parliament for the period of the war, to assume a watchful control over the government by parliament, and over parliament by the people, to demand the immediate removal of all political inequalities, since only a free people can adequately govern its country, and finally, to oppose to the imperialist war, based as it was upon the most reactionary forces in Europe, the program of Marx, of Engels, and Lassalle.

That was the flag that should have waved over the country. That would have been truly national, truly free, in harmony with the best traditions of Germany and the International class policy of the proletariat.

The great historical hour of the world war obviously demanded a unanimous political accomplishment, a broadminded, comprehensive attitude that only the Social-Democracy is destined to give. Instead, there followed, on the part of the parliamentary representatives of the working class, a miserable collapse. The Social-Democracy did not adopt the wrong policy—it had no policy whatsoever. It has wiped itself out completely as a class party with a world-conception of its own, has delivered the country, without a word of protest, to the fate of imperialistic war without, to the dictatorship of the sword within. Nay more, it has taken the responsibility for the war upon its own shoulders.

The declaration of the "Reichstag group" says: "We have voted only the means for our country's defense. We decline all responsibility for the war." But as a matter of fact, the truth lies in exactly the opposite direction. The means for "national defense," i. e., for imperialistic mass butchery by the armed forces of the military monarchy, were not voted by the Social-Democracy. For the availability of the war credits did not in the least depend upon the Social-Democracy. They, as a minority, stood against a compact three-quarters majority of the capitalist Reichstag. The Social-Democracy group accomplished only one thing by voting in favor of the war credits. It placed upon the war the stamp of democratic fatherland defense, and supported and sustained the fictions that were propagated by the government concerning the actual conditions and problems of the war.

Thus the serious dilemma between the national interests and international solidarity of the proletariat, the tragic conflict that made our parliamentarians fall "with heavy heart" to the side of imperialistic warfare, was a mere figment of the imagination, a bourgeois nationalist fiction. Between the national interests and the class interests of the proletariat, in war and in peace, there is actually complete harmony. Both demand the most energetic prosecution of the class struggle, and the most determined insistence on the Social-Democratic program.

But what action should the party have taken to give to our opposition to the war and to our war demands weight and emphasis? Should it have proclaimed a general strike? Should it have called upon the soldiers to refuse military service? Thus the question is generally asked. To answer with a simple yes or no, were just as ridiculous as to decide: "When war breaks out we will start a revolution." Revolutions are not "made" and great movements of the people are not produced according to technical recipes that repose in the pockets of the party leaders. Small circles of conspirators may organize a riot for a certain day and a certain hour, can give their small group of supporters the signal to begin. Mass movements in great historical crises cannot be initiated by such primitive measures. The best prepared mass strike may break down miserably at the very moment when the party leaders give the signal, may collapse completely before the first attack. The success of great popular movements depends, aye, the very time and circumstance of their inception is decided, by a number of economic, political and psychological factors. The existing degree of tension between the classes, the degree of intelligence of the masses and the degree or ripeness of their spirit of resistance—all these factors, which are incalculable, are premises that cannot be artificially created by any party. That is the difference between great historical upheavals, and the small show-demonstrations that a well disciplined party can carry out in times of peace, orderly, well-trained performances, responding obediently to the baton in the hands of the party leaders. The great historical hour itself creates the forms that will carry the revolutionary movement to a successful outcome, creates and improvises new weapons, enriches the arsenal of the people with weapons unknown and unheard of by the parties and their leaders.

What the Social-Democracy as the advance guard of the class-conscious proletariat should have been able to give was not ridiculous precepts and technical recipes, but a political slogan, clearness concerning the political problems and interests of the proletariat in times of war.

For what has been said of mass strikes in the Russian Revolution is equally applicable to every mass movement: "While the revolutionary period itself commands the creation and the computation and payment of the cost of a mass strike, the leaders of the Social-Democracy have an entirely different mission to fill. Instead of concerning itself with the technical mechanism of the mass movement, it is the duty of the Social-Democracy to undertake the political leadership even in the midst of a historical crisis. To give the slogan, to determine the direction of the struggle, to so direct the tactics of the political conflict that in its every phase and movement the whole sum of available and already mobilized active force of the proletariat is realized and finds expression in the attitude of the party, that the tactics of the Social-Democracy in determination and vigor shall never be weaker than is justified by the actual power at its back, but shall rather hasten in advance of its actual power, that is the important problem of the party leadership in a great historical crisis. Then this leadership will become, in a sense, the technical leadership. A determined, consistent, progressive course of action on the part of the Social-Democracy will create .in the masses assurance, self-confidence and a fearless fighting spirit. A weakly vacillating course, based upon a low estimate of the powers of the proletariat, lames and confuses the masses. In the first case mass action will break out "of its own accord" and "at the right time"; in the second even a direct call to action on the part of the leaders often remains ineffectual." (Rosa Luxemburg, "Mass Strike, Party and Labor Unions," Hamburg, 1907.)

Far more important that the outward, technical form of the action is its political content. Thus the parliamentary stage, for instance, the only far reaching and internationally conspicuous platform, could have become a mighty motive power for the awakening of the people, had it been used by the Social-Democratic representatives to proclaim loudly and distinctly, the interests, the problems and the demands of the working class.

"Would the masses have supported the Social-Democracy in its attitude against the war?" That is a question that no one can answer. But neither is it an important one. Did our parliamentarians demand an absolute assurance of victory from the generals of the Prussian army before voting in favor of war credits? What is true of military armies is equally true of revolutionary armies. They go into the fight, wherever necessity demands it, without previous assurance of success. At the worst, the party would have been doomed, in the first few months of the war, to political ineffectuality.

Perhaps the bitterest persecutions would have been inflicted upon our party for its manly stand, as they were, in 1870, the reward of Liebknecht and Bebel. "But what does that matter," said Ignatz Auer, simply, in his speech on the Sedanfeier in 1895. "A party that is to conquer the world must bear its principles aloft without counting the dangers that this may bring. To act differently is to be lost!"

"It is never easy to swim against the current," said the older Liebknecht, "And when the stream rushes on with the rapidity and the power of a Niagara it does not become easier! Our older comrades still remember the hatred of that year of greatest national shame, under the Socialist exception laws of 1878. At that time millions looked upon every Social-Democrat as having played the part of a murderer and a vile criminal in 1870; the Socialist had been in the eyes of the masses a traitor and an enemy. Such outbreaks of the "popular soul" are astounding, stunning, crushing in their elemental fury. One feels powerless, as before a higher power. It is a real force majeure. There is no tangible opponent. It is like an epidemic, in the people, in the air, everywhere.

"The outbreak of 1878 cannot, however, be compared with the outbreak in 1870. This hurricane of human passions, breaking, bending, destroying all that stands in its way—and with it the terrible machinery of militarism, in fullest, most horrible activity; and we stand between the crushing iron wheels, whose touch means instant death, between iron arms, that threaten every moment to catch us. By the side of this elemental force of liberated spirits stood the most complete mechanism of the art of murder the world had hitherto seen; and all in the wildest activity, every boiler heated to the bursting point. At such a time, what is the will and the strength of the individual? Especially, when one feels that one represents a tiny minority, that one possesses no firm support in the people itself.

"At that time our party was still in a period of development. We were placed before the most serious test, at a time when we did not yet possess the organization necessary to meet it. When the anti-socialist movement came in the year of shame of our enemies, in the year of honor for the Social-Democracy, then we had already a strong, widespread organization. Each and every one of us was strengthened by the feeling that he possessed a mighty support in the organized movement that stood behind him, and no sane person could conceive of the downfall of the party.

"So it was no small thing at that time to swim against the current. But what is to be done, must be done. And so we gritted our teeth in the face of the inevitable. There was no time for fear . . . Certainly Bebel and I . . . never for a moment thought of the warning. We did not retreat. We had to hold our posts, come what might!"

They stuck to their posts, and for forty years the Social-Democracy lived upon the moral strength with which it had opposed a world of enemies.

The same thing would have happened now. At first we would perhaps have accomplished nothing but to save the honor of the proletariat and thousands upon thousands of proletarians who are dying in the trenches in mental darkness, would not have died in spiritual confusion, but with the one certainty that that which has been everything in their lives, the international, liberating Social-Democracy, is more than the figment of a dream.

The voice of our party would have acted as a wet blanket upon the chauvinistic intoxication of the masses. It would have preserved the intelligent proletariat from delirium, would have made it more difficult for Imperialism to poison and to stupefy the minds of the people. The crusade against the Social-Democracy would have awakened the masses in an incredible short time.

And as the war went on, as the horror of endless massacre and bloodshed in all countries grew and grew, as its imperialistic hoof became more and more evident, as the exploitation by bloodthirsty speculators became more and more shameless, every live, honest, progressive and humane element in the masses would have rallied to the standard of the Social-Democracy. The German Social-Democracy would have stood in the midst of this mad whirlpool of collapse and decay, like a rock in a stormy sea, would have been the lighthouse of the whole International, guiding and leading the labor movements of every country of the earth. The unparalleled moral prestige that lay in the hands of the German Socialists would have reacted upon the Socialists of all nations in a very short time. Peace sentiments would have spread like wildfire and the popular demand for peace in all countries would have hastened the end of the slaughter, would have decreased the number of its victims.

The German proletariat would have remained the lighthouse-keeper of Socialism and of human emancipation.

Truly this was a task not unworthy of the disciples of Marx, Engels, and Lassalle.

CHAPTER VIII.

In spite of military dictatorship and press censorship, in spite of the downfall of the Social-Democracy, in spite of fratricidal war, the class struggle arises from civil peace with elemental force: from the blood and smoke of the battlefields the solidarity of international labor arises. Not in weak attempts to artificially galvanize the old International, not in pledges rendered now here, now there, to stand together after the war is over. No, here, in the war, out of the war arises, with a new might and intensity, the recognition that the proletarians of all lands have one and the same interest. The world war, itself, utterly disproves the falsehoods it has created.

Victory or defeat? It is the slogan of all-powerful militarism in every belligerent nation, and, like an echo, the social-democratic leaders have adopted it. Victory or defeat has become the highest motive of the workers of Germany, of France, of England and of others, just as for the ruling classes of these nations. When the cannons thunder, all proletarian interests subside before the desire for victory of their own, i. e., for defeat of the other countries. And yet, what can victory bring to the proletariat?

According to the official version of the leaders of the Social-Democracy, that was so readily adopted without criticism, victory of the German forces would mean, for Germany, unhampered, boundless industrial growth; defeat, however, industrial ruin. On the whole, this conception coincides with that generally accepted during the war of 1870. But the period of capitalist growth that followed the war of 1870 was not caused by the war, but resulted rather from the political union of the various German states, even though this union took the form of the crippled figure that Bismarck established as the German empire. Here the industrial impetus came from this union, in spite of the war and the manifold reactionary hindrances that followed in its wake. What the victorious war itself accomplished was to firmly establish the military monarchy and Prussian junkerdom in Germany; the defeat of France led to the liquidation of its Empire and the establishment of a Republic. But today the situation is different in all of the nations in question. Today war does not function as a dynamic force to provide for rising young capitalism the indispensable political conditions for its "national" development. Modern war appears in this role only in Serbia, and there only as an isolated fragment. Reduced to its objective historic significance, the present world war as a whole is a competitive struggle of a fully developed capitalism for world supremacy, for the exploitation of the last remnant of non-capitalistic world zones. This fact gives to the war and its political after effects an entirely new character. The high stage of world-industrial development in capitalistic production finds expression in the extraordinary technical development and destructiveness of the instruments of war, as in their practically uniform degree of perfection in all belligerent countries. The international organization of war industries is reflected in the military instability, that persistently brings back the scales, through all partial decisions and variations, to their true balance, and pushes a general decision further and further into the future. The indecision of military results, moreover, has the effect that a constant stream of new reserves, from the belligerent nations as well as from nations hitherto neutral, are sent to the front. Everywhere war finds material enough for imperialist desires and conflicts; itself creates new material to feed the conflagration that spreads out like a prairie fire. But the greater the masses, and the greater the number of nations that are dragged into this world-war, the longer will it rage. All of these things together prove, even before any military decision of victory or defeat can be established, that the result of the war will be: the economic ruin of all participating nations, and, in a steadily growing measure, of the formally neutral nations, a phenomenon entirely distinct from the earlier wars of modern times. Every month of war affirms and augments this effect, and thus takes away, in advance, the expected fruits of military victory for a decade to come. This, in the last analysis, neither victory nor defeat can alter; on the contrary it makes a purely military decision altogether doubtful, and increases the likelihood that the war will finally end through a general and extreme exhaustion. But even a victorious Germany, under such circumstances, even if its imperialistic war agitators should succeed in carrying on the mass murder to the absolute destruction of their opponents, even if their most daring dreams should be fulfilled—would win but a Pyrrhic victory. A number of annexed territories, impoverished and depopulated, and a grinning ruin under its own roof, would be its trophies. Nothing can hide this, once the painted stage properties of financial war-bond transactions, and the Potemkin villages of an "unalterable prosperity" kept up by war orders, are pushed aside. The most superficial observer cannot but see that even the most victorious nation cannot count on war indemnities that will stand in any relation to the wounds that the war has inflicted. Perhaps they may see in the still greater economic ruin of the defeated opponents, England and France, the very countries with which Germany was most closely united by industrial relations, upon whose recuperation its own prosperity so much depends, a substitute and an augmentation for their victory. Such are the circumstances under which the German people, even after a victorious war, would be required to pay, in cold cash, the war bonds that were "voted" on credit by the patriotic parliament; i. e., to take upon their shoulders an immeasurable burden of taxation, and a strengthened military dictatorship as the only permanent tangible fruit of victory.

Should we now seek to imagine the worst possible effects of

a defeat, we shall find that they resemble, line for line, with the exception of imperialistic annexations, the same picture that presented itself as the irrefutable consequence of victory: the effects of war today are so far reaching, so deeply rooted, that its military outcome can alter but little in its final consequences.

But let us assume, for the moment, that the victorious nation should find itself in the position to avoid the great catastrophe for its own people, should be able to throw the whole burden of the war upon the shoulders of its defeated opponent, should be able to choke off the industrial development of the latter by all sorts of hindrances. Can the German labor movement hope for successful development, so long as the activity of the French, English, Belgian and Italian laborers is hampered by industrial retrogression? Before 1870 the labor movements of the various nations grew independently of each other. The action of the nations grew, independently of each other. The action of the labor movement of a single city often controlled the destinies of the whole labor movement. On the streets of Paris the battles of the working class were fought out and decided. The modern labor movement, its laborious daily struggle in the industries of the world, its mass organization, are based upon the co-operation of the workers in all capitalistically producing countries. If the truism that the cause of labor can thrive only upon a virile, pulsating industrial life applies, then it is true not only for Germany, but for France, England, Belgium, Russia, and Italy as well. And if the labor movement in all of the capitalist states of Europe becomes stagnant, if industrial conditions there result in low wages, weakened labor unions, and a diminished power of resistance on the part of labor, labor unionism in Germany cannot possibly flourish. From this point of view the loss sustained by the working class in its industrial struggle is in the last analysis identical, whether German capital be strengthened at the expense of the French or English capital at the expense of the German.

But let us investigate the political effects of the war. Here differentiation should be less difficult than upon the economic side, for the sympathies and the partisanship of the proletariat have always tended toward the side that defended progress against reaction. Which side, in the present war, represents progress, which side reaction? It is clear that this question cannot be decided according to the outward insignias that mark the political character of the belligerent nations as "democracy" and absolutism. They must be judged solely according to the tendencies of their respective world policies.

Before we can determine what a German victory can win for the German proletariat we must consider its effect upon the general status of political conditions all over Europe. A decisive victory for Germany would mean, in the first place, the annexation of Belgium, as well as of a possible number of territories in the East and West and a part of the French colonies; the sustaining of the Hapsburg Monarchy and its aggrandizement by a number of new territories; finally the establishment of a fictitious "integrity" of Turkey, under a German protectorate—i. e., the conversion of Asia Minor and Mesopotamia, in one form or another, into German provinces. In the end this would result in the actual military and economic hegemony of Germany in Europe. Not because they are in accord with the desires of imperialist agitators are these consequences of an absolute German military victory to be expected, but because they are the inevitable outgrowth of the world-political position that Germany has adopted, of conflicting interests with England, France, and Russia, in which Germany has been involved, and which have grown, during the course of the war, far beyond their original dimensions. It is sufficient to recall these facts to realize that they could under no circumstances establish a permanent world-political equilibrium. Though this war may mean ruin for all of its participants, and worse for its defeated, the preparations for a new world war, under England's leadership, would begin on the day after peace is declared, to shake off the yoke of Prussian-German militarism that would rest upon Europe and Asia. A German victory would be the prelude to an early second world-war, and therefore, for this reason, but the signal for new feverish armaments, for the unleashing of the blackest reaction in every country, but particularly in Germany. On the other hand a victory of England or France would mean, in all likelihood, for Germany, the loss of a part of her colonies, as well as of Alsace-Lorraine, and certainly the bankruptcy of the world-political position of German militarism. But this would mean the disintegration of Austria-Hungary and the total liquidation of Turkey. Reactionary as both of these states are, and much as their disintegration would be in line with the demands of progressive development, in the present world-political milieu, the disintegration of the Hapsburg Monarchy and the liquidation of Turkey would mean the bartering of their peoples to the highest bidder—Russia, England, France, or Italy. This enormous redivision of the world and shifting of the balance of power in the Balkan states and along the Mediterranean would be followed inevitably by another in Asia: the liquidation of Persia and a redivision of China. This would bring the English-Russian as well as the English-Japanese conflict into the foreground of international politics, and may mean, in direct connection with the liquidation of the present war, a new world war, perhaps for Constantinople; would certainly bring it about, inescapably, in the immediate future. So a victory on this side, too, would lead to new, feverish armaments in all nations—defeated Germany, of course, at the head—and would introduce an era of undivided rule for militarism and reaction all over Europe, with a new war as its final goal.

So the proletariat, should it attempt to cast its influence into the balance on one side or the other, for progress or democracy, viewing the world policies in their widest application, would place itself between Scylla and Charybdis. Under the circumstances the question of victory or defeat becomes, for the European working class, in its political, exactly as in its economic aspects, a choice between two beatings. It is, therefore, nothing short of a dangerous madness for the French Socialists to believe that they can deal a death blow to militarism and imperialism, and clear the road for peaceful democracy, by overthrowing Germany. Imperialism, and its servant militarism, will reappear after every victory and after every defeat in this war. There can be but one exception: if the international proletariat, through its intervention, should overthrow all previous calculations.

The important lesson to be derived by the proletariat from this war is the one unchanging fact, that it can and must not become the uncritical echo of the "victory and defeat" slogan, neither in Germany nor in France, neither in England nor in Austria. For it is a slogan that has reality only from the point of view of imperialism, and is identical, in the eyes of every large power, with the question: gain or loss of world-political power, of annexations, of colonies, of military supremacy.

For the European proletariat as a class, victory or defeat of either of the two war groups would be equally disastrous. For war as such, whatever its military outcome may be, is the greatest conceivable defeat of the cause of the European proletariat. The overthrow of war, and the speedy forcing of peace, by the international revolutionary action of the proletariat, alone can bring to it the only possible victory. And this victory, alone, can truly rescue Belgium, can bring democracy to Europe.

For the class-conscious proletariat to identify its cause with either military camp is an untenable position. Does that mean that the proletarian policies of the present day demand a return to the "status quo," that we have no plan of action beyond the fond hope that everything may remain as it was before the war?

The existing conditions have never been our ideal, they have never been the expression of the self-determination of the people. And more, the former conditions cannot be reinstated, even if the old national boundaries should remain unchanged. For even before its formal ending this war has brought about enormous changes, in mutual recognition of one another's strength, in alliances, and in conflict. It has sharply revised the relations of countries to one another, of classes within society, has destroyed so many old illusions and portents, has created so many new forces and new problems, that a return to the old Europe that existed before August 4, 1914, is as impossible as the return to pre-revolutionary conditions, even after an unsuccessful revolution. The proletariat knows no going back, can only strive forward and onward, for a goal that lies beyond even the most newly created conditions. In this sense, alone, is it possible for the proletariat to oppose, with its policy, both camps in the imperialistic world war.

But this policy cannot concern itself with recipes for capitalist diplomacy worked out individually by the Social-Democratic parties, or even together in international conferences, to determine how capitalism shall declare peace in order to assure future peaceful and democratic development. All demands for complete or gradual disarmament, for the abolition of secret diplomacy, for the dissolution of the great powers into smaller national entities, and all other similar propositions, are absolutely utopian so long as capitalist class rule remains in power. For capitalism, in its present imperialistic course, to dispense with present-day militarism, with secret diplomacy, with the centralization of many national states, is so impossible that these postulates might, much more consistently, be united into the simple demand "abolition of capitalist class society." The proletarian movement cannot reconquer the place it deserves by means of utopian advice and projects for weakening, taming, or quelling imperialism within capitalism by means of partial reforms. The real problem that the world war has placed before the Socialist parties, upon whose solution the future of the working class movement depends, *is the readiness of the proletarian masses to act in the fight against imperialism*. The international proletariat suffers, not from a dearth of postulates, programs, and slogans, but from a lack of deeds, of effective resistance, of the power to attack imperialism at the decisive moment, just in times of war. It has been unable to put its old slogan, war against war, into actual practice. Here is the Gordian knot of the proletarian movement and of its future.

Imperialism, with all its brutal policy of force, with the incessant chain of social catastrophe that it itself provokes, is, to be sure, a historic necessity for the ruling classes of the present world. Yet nothing could be more detrimental than that the proletariat should derive, from the present war, the slightest hope or illusion of the possibility of an idyllic and peaceful development of capitalism. There is but one conclusion that the proletariat can draw from the historic necessity of imperialism. To capitulate before imperialism will mean to live forever in its shadow, off the crumbs that fall from the table of its victories

Historic development moves in contradictions, and for every necessity puts its opposite into the world as well. The capitalist state of society is doubtless a historic necessity, but so also is the revolt of the working class against it. Capital is a historic necessity, but in the same measure is its grave digger, the Socialist proletariat. The world rule of imperialism is a historic necessity, but likewise its overthrow by the proletarian international. Side by side the two historic necessities exist, in constant conflict with each other. And ours is the necessity of Socialism. Our necessity receives its justification with the moment when the capitalist class ceases to be the bearer of historic progress, when it becomes a hindrance, a danger, to the future development of society. That

capitalism has reached this stage the present world war has revealed.

Capitalist desire for imperialistic expansion, as the expression
of its highest maturity in the last period of its life, has the economic tendency to change the whole world into capitalistically
producing nations, to sweep away all superannuated, precapi-
talistic methods of production and of society, to subjugate all the
riches of the earth and all means of production to capital, to
turn the laboring masses of the peoples of all zones into wage
slaves. In Africa and in Asia, from the most northern regions
to the southernmost point of South America and in the South
Seas, the remnants of old communistic social groups, of feudal
society, of patriarchal systems, and of ancient handicraft production are destroyed and stamped out by capitalism. Whole peoples are destroyed, ancient civilizations are leveled to the ground,
and in their place profiteering in its most modern forms is being
established. This brutal triumphal procession of capitalism
through the world, accompanied by all the means of force, of
robbery, and of infamy, has one bright phase: It has created
the premises for its own final overthrow, it has established the
capitalist world rule upon which, alone, the Socialist world revolution can follow. This is the only cultural and progressive
aspect of the great so-called works of culture that were brought
to the primitive countries. To capitalist economists and politicians railroads, matches, sewerage systems and warehouses are
progress and culture. Of themselves such works, grafted upon
primitive conditions, are neither culture nor progress, for they
are too dearly paid for with the sudden economic and cultural
ruin of the peoples who must drink down the bitter cup of misery and horror of two social orders, of traditional agricultural
landlordism, of supermodern, superrefined capitalist exploitation,
at one and the same time. Only as the material conditions for
the destruction of capitalism and the abolition of class society

can the effects of the capitalist triumphal march through the world bear the stamp of progress in an historical sense. In this sense imperialism, too, is working in our interest.

The present world war is a turning point in the course of imperialism. For the first time the destructive beasts that have been loosed by capitalist Europe over all other parts of the world have sprung with one awful leap, into the midst of the European nations. A cry of horror went up through the world when Belgium, that priceless little jewel of European culture, when the venerable monuments of art in northern France, fell into fragments before the onslaughts of a blind and destructive force. The "civilized world" that had stood calmly by when this same imperialism doomed tens of thousands of heroes to destruction, when the desert of Kalahari shuddered with the insane cry of the thirsty and the rattling breath of the dying, when in Putumayo, within ten years, forty thousand human beings were tortured to death by a band of European industrial robber-barons, and the remnants of a whole people were beaten into cripples, when in China an ancient civilization was delivered into the hands of destruction and anarchy, with fire and slaughter, by the European soldiery, when Persia gasped in the noose of the foreign rule of force that closed inexorably about her throat, when in Tripoli the Arabs were mowed down, with fire and sword, under the yoke of capital, while their civilization and their homes were razed to the ground—this civilized world has just begun to know that the fangs of the imperialist beast are deadly, that its breath is frightfulness, that its tearing claws have sunk deep into the breasts of its own mother, European culture. And this belated recognition is coming into the world of Europe in the distorted form of bourgeois hypocrisy, that leads each nation to recognize infamy only when it appears in the uniform of the other. They speak of German barbarism, as if every people that goes out for organized murder did not change into a horde of barbarians! They speak of Cossack horrors, as if war itself

were not the the greatest of all horrors, as if the praise of human
slaughter in a Socialist periodical were not mental Cossackdom
in its very essence.

But the horrors of imperialist bestiality in Europe have had
another effect, that has brought to the "civilized world" no
horror-stricken eyes, no agonized heart. It is the mass destruction of the European proletariat. Never has a war killed off
whole nations; never, within the past century, has it swept over
all of the great and established lands of civilized Europe. Millions
of human lives were destroyed in the Vosges, in the Ardennes, in
Belgium, in Poland, in the Carpathians and on the Save; millions
have been hopelessly crippled. But nine-tenths of these millions
come from the ranks of the working class of the cities and the
farms. It is our strength, our hope that was mowed down there,
day after day, before the scythe of death. They were the best, the
most intelligent, the most thoroughly schooled forces of international socialism, the bearers of the holiest traditions, of the
highest heroism, the modern labor movement, the vanguard of
the whole world proletariat, the workers of England, France,
Belgium, Germany and Russia who are being gagged and
butchered in masses. Only from Europe, only from the oldest
capitalist nations, when the hour is ripe, can the signal come for
the social revolution that will free the nations. Only the English, the French, the Belgian, the German, the Russian, the Italian
workers, together, can lead the army of the exploited and oppressed. And when the time comes they alone can call capitalism
to account for centuries of crime committed against primitive
peoples; they alone can avenge its work of destruction over a
whole world. But for the advance and victory of Socialism we
need a strong, educated, ready proletariat, masses whose strength
lies in knowledge as well as in numbers. And these very masses
are being decimated all over the world. The flower of our youth-
ful strength, hundreds of thousands whose socialist education in
England, in France, in Belgium, in Germany and in Russia was

the product of decades of education and propaganda, other hundreds of thousands who were ready to receive the lessons of Socialism, have fallen, and are rotting upon the battlefields. The fruit of the sacrifices and toil of generations is destroyed in a few short weeks, the choicest troops of the international proletariat are torn out by the life roots.

The blood-letting of the June battle laid low the French labor movement for a decade and a half. The blood-letting of the Commune massacre again threw it back for more than a decade. What is happening now is a massacre such as the world has never seen before, that is reducing the laboring population in all of the leading nations to the aged, the women and the maimed; a blood-letting that threatens to bleed white the European labor movement.

Another such war, and the hope of Socialism will be buried under the ruins of imperialistic barbarism. That is more than the ruthless destruction of Liége and of the Rheims Cathedral. That is a blow. not against capitalist civilization of the past, but against Socialist civilization of the future, a deadly blow against the force that carries the future of mankind in its womb, that alone can rescue the precious treasures of the past over into a better state of society. Here capitalism reveals its death's head, here it betrays that it has sacrificed its historic right of existence, that its rule is no longer compatible with the progress of humanity.

But here is proof also that the war is not only a grandiose murder, but the suicide of the European working class. The soldiers of socialism, the workers of England, of France, of Germany, of Italy, of Belgium are murdering each other at the bidding of capitalism, are thrusting cold, murderous irons into each others' breasts, are tottering over their graves, grappling in each others' death-bringing arms.

"Deutschland, Deutschland über alles," "long live democracy," "long live the czar and slavery," "ten thousand tent cloths, guaranteed according to specifications," "hundred thousand pounds of bacon," "coffee substitute, immediate delivery . . . dividends are rising—proletarians falling; and with each one there sinks a fighter of the future, a soldier of the revolution, a savior of humanity from the yoke of capitalism, into the grave.

This madness will not stop, and this bloody nightmare of hell will not cease until the workers of Germany, of France, of Russia and of England will wake up out of their drunken sleep; will clasp each other's hands in brotherhood and will drown the bestial chorus of war agitators and the hoarse cry of capitalist hyenas with the mighty cry of labor, "Proletarians of all countries, unite!"